PASSIVE INCOME IDEAS AND NO MORE PROCRASTINATION

2-in-1 Book

Latest Reliable & Most Profitable Business Ideas to Make $10,000/month + Simple Habits to Boost Your Productivity and Overcome Laziness

PASSIVE INCOME IDEAS

Latest Reliable & Profitable Business Ideas. Make $10,000/month with Affiliate Marketing, Blogging, Dropshipping, Amazon FBA, and More

Table of Contents

Introduction 7

Chapter 1—A Beginner's Passive Income.. 10
Four Types of Passive Income... 11
Five Quick-Start Steps for Passive Income 14
Five Genius Micro-Investing Tools 22

Chapter 2--Discover Self-Publishing Success...................................... 27
How to Write A Book. Your Road Toward Making Big Bucks in Self-Publishing... 31
Marketing Your Book. Tips for Maximizing Your Book Profits 41
Tips for Publishing Audio Books... 43
Six Steps Toward Earning Extra Income by Publishing Online Courses 46

Chapter 3--Blogging for Big Profits.. 52
The Truth About Earning Through Blogs... 52
Seven Ways to Earn Income from Blogging 58

Chapter 4—Make Passive Income on the Internet Now 63
All You Need to Know About Affiliate Marketing................................ 63
Five Steps Toward Becoming an Affiliate Marketer.............................. 65
Make Money Dropshipping 72
Five Essential Steps in Creating Dropshipping Business 73

Chapter 5—Get Richer While You Sleep... 76
Amazon FBA 76
All You Need to Know About Peer-to-Peer Lending Opportunities 78

40 Ways You Can Use Your Skills or Interests to Earn Passive Income 81

Chapter 6--Make Killer Investments **89**

How to Start Investing in Stocks *89*

All About CD Laddering *94*

Four Simple Ways to Make Real Estate Investment Income *95*

Conclusion **99**

Introduction

Let's look into some reasons why you're interested in finding some additional income streams. Maybe you already have a job, but the money you earn from that job never seems to provide enough income to meet all your wants and needs. Or maybe you're making enough income to fulfill your current wants and needs, but you can't imagine working the job you're working now forever. You'd like to transition into a career or careers which offer you more independence, more flexibility, more income, or all of the above. Or maybe you're looking for a way to supplement your current income without spending a lot of time to do so. You're not necessarily looking for "easy money", but it would be nice if you could supplement your income without having to allocate a lot of time to do so.

In this book, I'm going to provide you with the information you'll need to create additional income streams for yourself without having to spend a lot of extra time to do so. You may have heard people boast about making money while they sleep. Well, passive income streams can allow you to do exactly that—make money while you are sleeping. Yes, there will be some initial effort required, but I'll show you some ways to make additional income with minimal effort. In some instances, you'll be able to use your money to make more money. On the other hand, if you don't have the money required to make more money, I'll show you some other ways you can increase your income streams with little or no financial investment. So, if you have the money to make more money, but not the time, I can help you. Likewise, if you have the time but not the money to make more money, I can help you.

My name is David Allen. I call myself a "side hustle" expert. For years, I researched and tried many different ways to create additional income for myself and my family. I've made it my mission in life to find easy and practical ways to make additional income. During my journey, I've developed some tried and true ways for people to make extra income. And yes, I've made some mistakes along the way. But I'm always happy to have others learn from my mistakes and missteps. As I grew older, I've found that my mistakes are fewer and further in between. I'm now at a point where I think I have a lot of good information to share with others. I've proven that I can set up some great passive income streams, many of which require very little time and effort.

In the past, I've imparted many of my findings to friends who were eager to learn how to make more passive income. Many of those friends have benefitted substantially from my knowledge and experience in setting up their own passive income streams. Some of them even credit me for changing their lives; many of them have often encouraged me to write this book and share my vast knowledge with others who are looking to improve their own financial status. I'm hoping that you'll be one of the people who benefit immensely from my knowledge and expertise.

With the information I provide, you will be able to create additional income streams for yourself. You'll be able to earn or save extra money immediately with some of the ideas I provide. Other income streams may take slightly longer, but for the most part, you should be able to start earning extra income without spending a lot of time working on it. As you read this book, you'll note that there are many different means of earning additional income. You'll have to determine which of these income streams will work for you. And once you determine that, you will be well on your way toward earning some additional income through the many different streams available to you.

Since you're reading this book, I'm assuming that you'd probably like to start earning extra income sooner than later. With this in mind, I encourage you to start to change your life now by implementing some of the tips and techniques I'm offering. In writing a self-help book like this, there's always the danger that the reader will subscribe to the ideas offered, but then resolve to implement them later. As we all know, many times, people who resolve to implement the changes later will place the ideas on the back burner and then never get back to them. With this in mind, I'd like to encourage you to start implementing these ideas today. After all, why wait to make changes which will allow you to earn additional income and set you on the road to financial independence? Unless you're independently wealthy, I'm sure you'll be happy to start earning some extra income immediately.

The tips and techniques I provide can yield incredible results, if only you'll take the time to implement them. Every chapter in this book should help you in your efforts to create additional income streams without spending a lot of time in implementing or maintaining these streams. By the time you finish reading this book, you'll know all about passive income streams and how they can change your life. Together, we can make it happen.

Chapter 1—A Beginner's Passive Income

Before I can start telling you how you might start earning passive income, I'd like to first define the term "passive income" and tell you how it is different from other forms of income.

Some of you may have heard the mantra, "Make Money While You Sleep". This concept is often paralleled with the concept of passive income.

Passive income is income resulting from cash flow received on a regular basis—with little or no effort or participation on the part of the recipient. Although I wouldn't classify passive income as "easy money", I'll point out that many passive income streams offer opportunities for people to make money without a lot of effort. Yes, some effort may be required at the outset of any passive income opportunity. However, after that initial effort, many passive income streams allow the recipients to derive income on a continuous basis without a lot of participation, effort, or maintenance.

The U.S. Internal Revenue Service lists three categories of income: active income, passive income, and portfolio income. I'll offer a brief description of each income category so we can keyhole the passive income category we'll be focusing on in this book.

Active income is the income a person earns from standard jobs or a mainstream career. If you're a restaurant waiter, a marketing executive, a nurse, or a teacher…any standard career, the salary you earn in doing that job is considered active income. It's called active income because you are active at earning that income. For example, if you are a restaurant waiter, and you decide not to go to work for a couple of weeks, it's likely that you won't get paid or won't derive any income from that job. You'll only earn income from the job if you are active at it.

You may have heard people previously refer to their main jobs as their "A" jobs and their side venture or side hustle jobs as their "B" jobs. When people refer to their "A" jobs, they are almost always referring to active income jobs in which they derive a steady income resulting from their participation in that career. And many people use the income from their "A" job to get into the two other categories of income—passive income and portfolio income.

Portfolio income is income derived from activities such as investments, dividends, interest, capital gains, and royalties. Portfolio income is not earned through regular business activity. Portfolio income is not derived from passive income investments and is not earned through regular business activity.

Passive income, the type of income we'll be focusing on with this book, is income that is derived regularly from activities that require little or no effort or participation on the part of the recipient. As I've already pointed out, passive income isn't always "easy money" or "money made while sleeping", as many passive income activities require at least some initial effort on the behalf of the person who hopes to benefit. And many passive income activities require some ongoing maintenance to remain successful.

Four Types of Passive Income

Before we start telling you some ways you can earn passive income, let's explain the four types of passive income activities, how they work, and how they are different from each other. Here are the four types of passive income activities:

Passive Income Ideas

1) **Use Cash to Buy Cash-Flowing Assets.** This is the "use money to make money" approach. Now, before you get discouraged, we realize that not all of you have the money required to participate in this option. For those of you that don't, other very viable options which don't require cash will follow. But for those of you that have money to use in increasing your assets, you'll be able to do things such as real estate investments, dividend investing, and business lending to increase your passive income earnings. That said, many people who have the "money to make money" find that they don't have the time to put their money to work for them. With this in mind, I'll provide you with some recommendations on how you can use your money to make more money without allocating a lot of extra time to do so.

2) **Build Cash-Flowing Assets.** If you don't have mountains of investable cash available, don't despair. You're not alone. You can still build your passive income earnings. Many people have increased their passive income earnings, spending little or no money. Some have built digital products or websites. Others have developed blogs, comparison shopping concepts, affiliate marketing concepts, or even online teaching courses to create ongoing income streams. Although most of these activities require some initial time and effort, they can provide income streams that will last for a long time, without any upfront expenditures.

3) **Sell or Share Assets.** Do you have assets that you own or control that you can turn into passive income streams? If you'll look around, you can probably identify some tangible assets that could be sold or shared to produce additional income. For example, do you have an exercise bike that you're no longer using and it's just taking up space in your garage? That's an item you could probably sell to earn

some extra income. Do you have a car and some extra time to drive around? If so, you can earn some passive income by becoming an Uber or a Lyft driver. Did you collect baseball cards as a kid? Maybe it's time to sell those cards. Do you have an extra bedroom in your house? Maybe you could rent out that extra room. Do you have an empty shed on your property? Maybe you could rent this shed out as a storage space. In all likelihood, you already have assets there that can be turned into cash. Look around and see what assets you already own or control. You'll almost certainly find that some of these assets can be turned into passive income streams.

4) Reverse Passive Income. With this passive income activity, you'll be saving money instead of making money. You'll do so by reducing your ongoing expenses. For example, you could reduce your cable TV bill by renegotiating it or having a negotiating service do that for you. Even if you only negotiate a savings of $20 per month, that will amount to $240 annually. You could also negotiate interest rates on credit cards or switch to credit cards that have better rates or attractive introductory offers. If you are storing some of your belongings in a storage facility, can you get rid of some of the contents of that unit so you can then rent a smaller, less expensive unit? You get the picture…look at your monthly expenses and see if there is a way you could reduce some of those expenses to save money. That's reverse passive income. And even though this activity will not make you more money, it will allow you to save some money that can certainly be used to make more money.

Five Quick-Start Steps for Passive Income

We're going to get going with some ideas for you to start making some quick passive income. Most of the following ideas are offered with the idea that they'll not require a lot of initial startup or setup time. Ideas on more time-intensive passive income streams will follow later in this book. My goal is to get you started immediately with some passive income streams that require very little time. Then, once you realize that you can indeed derive income from these streams, you can proceed to more complex streams that require more startup time.

1)   Credit Cards. As most people have credit cards, and many of those people use credit cards for their ongoing purchases, let's start with how you can derive passive income from your credit cards.

There are a number of things you can do with your credit cards to ensure that you get the maximum passive income from those cards.

The first thing you should consider is the charges that accompany your credit cards. This includes annual fees and interest rates. It's my feeling that you should never pay an annual fee for a credit card that you are using on a regular basis unless the benefits and rewards you receive from having that card substantially outweigh the annual fee. Annual credit card fees will range from $25 to $500 per card. There are plenty credit cards out there that advertise no annual fees and if your credit card company is charging you an annual fee, I suggest that you either consider a switch to another credit card company or call your current credit card company and ask them to waive your annual fee. You should know that almost all credit card companies are open to waiving the annual fees, especially for the first year.

Next, you should find out what the interest rates are on your credit cards and then compare your rate with the rates offered by other credit card companies. If you pay off the full balance on your card every month, the interest rate you get on your card won't matter much, however if you have a continuous balance on that card that you're not able to pay off completely every month, then your interest rate should be a major consideration and you should compare your existing rate with rates offered by other cards. There are many sites on the internet that compare credit card rates, and you should be able to easily compare your rates with other rates with the simple click of a mouse. Again, if your current interest rate is not to your liking but you like your credit card company, you should consider calling your credit card company and asking them to reduce your rate to a more competitive level. Yes, it's possible that they might not accommodate your request, but the worst that can happen is that they say "no". Then if your card rate is not competitive, you can consider switching credit card companies.

Another consideration with credit cards is the benefits or rewards you receive with your card. Does your card offer a cashback program? If so, what is the cashback percentage rate and how does that compare to other cards? Or do you have a travel rewards card? If you do, make sure you plan to utilize the travel miles that are accumulating, before they expire. I've known people who have credit cards with travel rewards that are no longer travelers. For these people, they would be better suited to a credit card that offers rewards other than travel miles. Some credit cards offer gift cards as rewards. Again, you should compare those cards with other cashback or gift card rewards to make sure your credit card company is competitive. If not, consider a switch to another credit card company.

2) **Rewards Programs.** Another way to enhance your earning power is to enroll in rewards programs at places where you regularly

shop. For example, my supermarket chain has a rewards program in which I receive periodic discounts on items I purchase and regular discounts on gas purchases at their service station. When I enrolled in this program, I registered online in less than five minutes. I don't have to carry a plastic card in my wallet; I just give them my phone number whenever I make a purchase. On average, I save 20 to 30 cents per gallon at their service station every time I refuel my car. In a similar vein, I buy office supplies for my small business at Office Max, and they also have a rewards program in which all I have to do is give them my phone number whenever I make a purchase. This rewards program accumulates cash rewards that I can use for future purchases.

Also, there are apps such as Drop, which allow people to earn discounts from their top five retailers. You get to choose your favorite retailers and then you accumulate rewards points with each purchase you make from these five retailers. (Even Lyft and Uber are among the businesses you can choose among your five favorites.) The reward points you accumulate can eventually be redeemed as gift cards from major retailers including Amazon, Starbucks, Groupon, etc. Again, registration is simple and free. You'll be registering retailers that you already purchase from, so it's a can't-lose proposition.

3) Savings Accounts, Checking Accounts. Most people have checking accounts and some people have savings accounts. With all of your bank accounts, I suggest that you verify what your interest rates are for those accounts and then compare them with the rates you might receive from other banks. Again, we have to understand that many people choose their banks for convenience reasons. So if the competing banks' interest rates are only slightly higher than that of your bank's, these higher rates may not merit a switch. However, if they are substantially higher, then you might consider a switch or contact your current bank and ask them if they have any other programs that can be made available to you to raise the rates you're receiving. Please know that interest rates on checking accounts are seldom high and you're probably not going to get rich by trying to negotiate rates or switching to another bank. Nevertheless, "a penny saved is a penny earned" and you can decide if a switch or negotiation is worth it.

Just as important in considering your banking expenses are the fees that you'll pay from your bank. As we all know, banks are well-known for fees that are a major source of their revenue and some banks have even been accused of gouging customers with their fees. In evaluating your bank, I strongly suggest that you analyze the fees they charge. Each bank should be able to supply you with a list of fees. Those fees may even be posted on the bank's website. Does your checking account have a monthly maintenance fee? Is there a minimum balance amount before fees are applied? Do you ever have overdrafts? If so, what are their charges? Many banks have overdraft protection programs they can offer you. Many people take these bank charges for granted when it would behoove them to review these charges at least annually to make sure they are competitive with charges and fees from other banks.

Although reviewing, shopping, or negotiating bank fees may not be the most exciting way to make money and may not make you a millionaire, it is something easy that you can do in very little time to make or save you money on a monthly basis.

4) **Certificates of Deposit.** If you're fortunate enough to have enough money to maintain certificates of deposit, I suggest you "shop" interest rates with banks before depositing funds or renewing certificates. As certificates of deposit don't require much attention, it is not unusual for certificate holders to use banks other than their regular banks. Convenience for certificates of deposit is not a factor that it is for checking accounts, as you basically deposit the funds for your certificates of deposit and then the money just stays in the bank for the term of the certificate. So, don't hesitate to shop interest rates with your certificates of deposit.

5) **Rent Your Assets.** Most of us have at least some rentable assets from which we could derive passive income. Do you have a car? A boat? A vacation home? A recreational vehicle? An empty shed or garage stall? A spare room in your home? All of these assets could provide some passive income streams.

a) **Your house or your spare room.** If you're willing to rent out your house or even a spare room in your house, you can make some serious cash. Airbnb and other similar sites provide reliable vehicles for you to rent out your home. I have friends in Minneapolis that rented out their home for Super Bowl week and, in doing so, they earned enough money to pay their mortgage for an entire year. They earned five figures per night. Yes, they have a nice home, but this will give you an idea of how much money can be raised in renting a house or even a spare room.

Now, it's important to remember that the Super Bowl brings over 100,000 visitors to town and there are not enough hotel rooms to accommodate all the visitors. So, the market is ripe for the picking during that time. Companies like Airbnb will do the background checks on your guests and they will also collect the rental fee you have requested. So, there is very little work on your part except to prepare the home for visitors. My friends who rented out their home for the

Super Bowl made arrangements to stay with relatives during the week they had their house rented.

I have another group of friends that similarly rented out their home in a suburb of Minneapolis for the Ryder Cup golf event, which is an international golf event that is extremely popular, almost as popular as the Super Bowl. Likewise, they were able to pay an entire year's mortgage by renting their house to the family of one of the professional golfers participating in the event. Again, what you can rent your home for will depend on the quality of your home and the popularity of the event in your area, but there is substantial money to be made in renting out your home to visitors, whether they are in your city for a major sporting event, a major concert event, a major political convention, etc. Another Minnesota friend of mine rented out his apartment to a member of the news media who was attending the Republican Convention in nearby St. Paul. Again, there were no hotel rooms available and my friend's apartment was on a light-rail train route with easy access to the convention center in St. Paul where the event was being held.

Do you have a vacation home that sits empty for most of the year? I have a lake home on a secluded lake in northern Minnesota. I use that lake home only about five weeks out of every year. With this in mind, I have started renting out this lake home to interested parties. I, of course, block out the periods in which I am going to be using the lake home, but the home is open for rental at all other times. I used a third-party service to manage my bookings, to correspond with the guests, and to do the cleanings before the guests arrive and after they leave. My participation in the entire activity is mostly centered around accepting the money which the management company collects. (Yes, it's a tough job, but someone has to do it!) I've found this to be an extremely profitable side venture and I've noticed that I have a smile on my face every time I deposit one of the checks from this activity.

One more thought on a far more basic level: If you have a spare bedroom or bedrooms in your home that is mostly being used as a junk room, you might consider renting out this room on either a temporary or an ongoing basis. If you do this, you should obviously make sure you vet or do a background check on your prospective renter. You won't want to grant access to your house to a complete stranger. But if you can find a trustworthy person to rent your spare room, it may well be worth the additional income you'll derive from this passive income activity. As an example, I have a family member who has a small spare bedroom in his family's home. They cleaned all of the junk out of their spare bedroom and rented it to a college kid who had a summer internship in their city. Since it was a small bedroom and since their renter was a cash-strapped college kid, the renters didn't get rich from renting the spare bedroom. Nonetheless, they earned some extra income which they appreciated and they convinced the college kid to mow the lawn in the months he was renting.

b) **Your boat or your recreational vehicle.** Along the same lines, if you own a boat or a recreational vehicle (RV), you're probably not using the boat or the RV on a continual basis. In fact, most boat and RV owners use those items only a couple of times a year. These are expensive assets that can be turned into passive revenue streams. Companies such as Boatsetter and GetMyBoat are vehicles in which you can rent out your boat. Companies such as RVShare and Outdoorsy are available for peer-to-peer RV rentals. If you'll browse those sites, you will get a good idea of how much you can rent your boat or RV for. Your boat rental fee will depend on a number of factors, including how large it is and where it is located. Your RV rental fee will depend on similar factors. It is not unusual for an RV rental to bring a $150 to $300 rental per day. Again, the companies that are in this boat rental or RV rental business will often provide the insurance on the boat or the vehicle. At the same time, they will do background checks on the prospective renters and they will collect the rental fee. They'll then take their cut of the action and pay you the remaining amount.

c) **Your car.** The average vehicle sits idle for 22 hours a day. Many families own more than one car. Cars are another asset which you can use to make passive income. Companies such as Turo and Getaround offer peer-to-peer car rental platforms. These companies allow you to set the rental price for your vehicle and, importantly, they handle the vetting for the people who want to rent your car and they also handle the insurance for these rentals.

Another way to use your car as an income stream is to become a driver in your spare time. Most of you are familiar with well-known enterprises such as Uber or Lyft. With these companies, it is a relatively simple process to become accepted as one of their drivers and they offer you the flexibility of driving only when you have the spare time to drive. It's a good way to make extra cash. I have friends who are Uber or Lyft drivers in their spare time and they then use the money they earn to make their monthly car payments or their car insurance payments.

Finally, if you're not picky about what your car looks like, you can opt to make it a mobile billboard. Companies like Wrapify will pay you to use your car as a mobile billboard and to advertise various products or services. The money you make in doing this will depend on where you live (highly-populated areas are preferred) and how many miles you drive. Wrapify and other companies like it will track your mileage and then pay you accordingly. It's not unheard of for people to make $100 a week for their mobile billboards.

Five Genius Micro-Investing Tools

I'll admit that until a couple of years ago, I didn't even know what micro-investing was. For those of you who are not familiar with the concept, I'll give you a quick lesson in what it is and how it works. Micro-investing is an activity in which people can invest small amounts in stock. Micro-investing almost always occurs through mobile platforms or apps. Unlike traditional modes of stock investing, micro-investing is not restricted to people who have lots of money. Investments are often very minimal, as the name micro indicates, and investors can usually invest with as little as $1 to $5 at a time. Micro-investing is designed to remove the traditional roadblocks to investing by beginning investors, including brokerage minimums.

With micro-investing, you will not need to become a stock market wonk. As a matter of fact, you won't need to know anything about the stock market. Most of the micro-investing apps will select portfolios for you, based on your preferences, and then they'll place the small amounts you're investing into those funds. When you first start on a micro-investing app, they'll ask you to fill out a questionnaire so they can determine your preferences and then cater your investments toward your preferences.

Passive Income Ideas

One thing I really like about many of the micro-investing apps is that they have automatic means for you to make your small investments. Some of those means are described below under the descriptions of the individual apps.

Although no one would say that you'll become a multi-millionaire by micro-investing and no one would ever proport that you'll become the next Warren Buffett, micro-investing is a good way to get your feet wet in the stock market without laying out or risking a lot of cash. You'll be able to make or save small amounts of money without a major cash outlay and without broker's minimums and fees.

As you might imagine, there are quite a few micro-investing apps to choose from. I'll outline a few of these apps below, but you should note that there are always new apps coming out that you may want to look into if you are interested in micro-investing.

1) **Acorns.** This is one of the most popular apps, as it allows you to invest very small amounts by automatically rounding your debit and credit card charges to the nearest higher dollar amount and then it invests this small extra amount (always less than $1) for you. For example, if I buy a toner cartridge for my printer and the cost of that cartridge is $24.39, Acorns will round the charge up to $25 and add the 61 cents change to my investment account. If for whatever reason, you don't want these amounts invested automatically, you can manually select for which charges these small extra amounts can be invested. The thing I like about this site automatically rounding my charges to the next highest dollar amount is that I consider these small amounts to be pocket change which will have very little impact on my bank account and which I'm never going to miss. But with all the debit and credit charges I make, those small amounts add up to a decent investment account over a period of time.

To give you an idea as to the amount of money I can save and invest with the Acorns app, I've been averaging over $40 per month saved and invested. Admittedly, I use my debit and credit cards quite frequently, because I use them for personal purchases and for my small business purchases (and I rarely pay cash for the items I purchase), but this will give you an idea as to what you might expect to earn on the Acorns app. I project that my annual savings/investments will total somewhere between $450 and $500 annually. No, that won't put me in the same tax category as Amazon founder Jeff Bezos, but $500 isn't chump change either, at least not for me.

Acorns charges $1 a month for its services, money that I easily get back from my investments. As mentioned before, they'll ask you a few questions when you register with them and they'll use the information you provide to create a financial profile for you. They'll then build your investment portfolio, which can range from conservative to aggressive, depending on the information you give them on your questionnaire.

2) **Stash.** Stash is a bit different than Acorns, as it is slightly more hands-on for investors. With this app, instead of adding to your debit and credit card charges, Stash is set up so you can withdraw a specified amount from your bank account each week or each month. Like Acorns, Stash will ask you a set of questions in an effort to determine whether they should steer you toward conservative, moderate, or aggressive investments. Once they have determined this, they will provide you with a set of simple portfolios in which you can choose to

invest. Again, you'll not need to be a stock expert to determine which stocks you'll invest in, but you'll at least be required to choose a preference, something you won't have to do with Acorns. Stash has a $1 monthly fee and they require that you've accumulated a minimum of $5 before you can start investing.

3)   **Rize.** Rize is a goal-oriented savings and investment app. The savings component of this app is designed to help you save the amounts of money you want in order to pay for things you want. For example, if you want to get a new surfboard at a cost of about $400, Rize will set you up on a savings program in which they will designate a specified amount of each of your paychecks toward this purchase. (You'll be the one who specifies the amount to be deducted from each paycheck.) At the same time, you tell them how much money you'll need to purchase a new surfboard, you'll also tell them when you'd like to have this surfboard. With this app, you can easily adjust your settings at any time. You can accelerate or decelerate your payments, if necessary. Rize charges an annual management fee of 0.25% on your investments. Some of these fees are offset by the 1.6% interest they pay on your balance.

4)   **Robinhood.** The Robinhood app is an app for buying and selling stocks on U.S. exchanges. The app can also be used to buy and sell ETFs (exchange-traded funds) and cryptocurrencies. This program is well-known because it is free and it doesn't charge any of the fees that are typically associated with stock transactions. No commissions, no account maintenance fees, no trading fees. On the other hand, the Robinhood app is a bare-bones app which does not offer investment advice or research. If you're interested in buying or selling stocks on this app, you'll have to get your advice elsewhere.

5) Betterment. Unlike Robinhood, Betterment allows you to be hands-off with your investments. It also gives you access to financial advisors who can offer investment advice through the app's messaging system. Betterment has two tiers: The Betterment Digital tier is available with no required account minimum. Betterment charges 0.25% of assets for its Digital tier. The company also offers Betterment Premium at 0.40% of assets with a minimum investment of $100,000. With Betterment Premium, the company offers unlimited phone access to members. I realize that Betterment Premium will not be viable to most of us here, but the Betterment Digital tier is a good deal if you are interested to buy and sell stocks and to be able to solicit the advice of their financial advisors throughout the process.

Chapter 2--Discover Self-Publishing Success

Self-publishing is one of the most popular forms of earning passive income. Before I tell you how to discover self-publishing success, I want to make sure you understand what self-publishing is. In the days before the internet, if you wanted to write a book and have it published, you were either totally at the discretion of traditional publishers or you had to pay to have large quantities of your own book printed. Authors who wanted to have their own books printed, probably because they couldn't sell them to publishers, often had to purchase as many as 5000 books in order to get a reasonable price.

In those days, a friend of mine who eventually became a New York Times best-selling author had always had the dream to be an author. After he finished writing his first book, he submitted it to 27 different publishers. He received 27 letters of rejection. He believed in his book and his writing abilities so sincerely that he decided to go the "vanity press" route and have his book printed without a publisher. He had to print 5000 books at that time, and, as a student recently out of college and a person who held a bartending job to pay the bills, he didn't have anything close to the money he needed to print the 5000-book minimum. He was a great salesman and he eventually secured the funds needed through loans from some of his bar patrons.

He had the 5000 books printed and then loaded up the trunk of his car with boxes of his books and drove from bookstore to bookstore in an effort to hawk his books. As I mentioned before, he was a great salesman and he was eventually able to sell all 5000 of his political thriller books to bookstores and individuals. Soon after he reordered his second batch of books, he received a call from a publisher who had been tracking his book purchases from the "vanity press". That publisher asked him to submit a manuscript and soon after that, my friend was offered his first book contract from a publisher. He went on to make a career of it and he wrote six New York Times bestsellers before he, unfortunately, died of cancer at an early age.

I tell you this story of how things used to be so I can illustrate how things have changed since the advent of the internet and digital printers. Now you can write a book, you can load it to an online self-publishing site, and you can sell digital books, printed books, or audiobooks. Most impressively, you can purchase printed books in minimum quantities of one. Yes, you read that right. You can have one book printed at a time. As a matter of fact, with digital printers, your printed book will not be printed until someone orders it online. Then the printer will ship that book within a matter of days, instead of the matter of weeks or months required for printing in the days before the internet.

Although there are quite a few steps involved in writing and self-publishing a book, the process is now so much easier than it ever was before and it can be done very inexpensively. In this book chapter, I'm going to tell you how to write and publish your own books. Publishing your own books is one of the most popular ways for people to earn passive income.

There are a ton of success stories about people who have made a fortune through self-publishing their own books.

Accurate statistics on the book industry aren't always easy to find, but I have some statistics that will show you what a huge market the book market is. According to the NPD Group (National Purchase Diary), a well-known American market research firm, over 696 million printed books were sold in 2018. According to Data Guy, a renowned book industry analyst, over 781 million eBooks were sold from April 2017 through September 2018, totaling a sales amount of $4.02 billion. This should give you a good idea of what you'll be getting into when you decide to self-publish books.

Before we get further along, I should probably define eBooks for those of you who may not be quite sure what the term encompasses. The term eBook is short for electronic book, and it includes all books that can be read on mobile devices such as cell phones and tablets, computers, and eBook devices such as Kindle and Nook.

When you self-publish your books, you are going to have to decide if you want printed books, ebooks, audiobooks, or all of the above. It's very common now for people to publish printed and eBook versions of the same book. Audiobooks are not quite as popular, but they are quickly rising in popularity and they offer yet another vehicle for you to get your book out there for people who prefer listening to books instead of reading them.

Probably the biggest success story in e-publishing is the story of author E.L. James and her *50 Shades of Gray* series. She published her first book in that series in 2011 as an eBook and a print-on-demand paperback. Her books have now sold over a million copies, including books that have now been turned into movies.

Self-publishing success stories are abundant on the internet. I'll take the time to give you one woman's story because it's a great success story and it will give you an idea of the possibilities that self-publishing can offer. Admittedly, very few people will ever achieve these lofty levels, but it's nice to dream, isn't it? Amanda Hocking was an unknown author from Minnesota who couldn't get published by a traditional publisher. She worked a day job as a group home caregiver to pay the bills and then wrote paranormal novels in her spare time. Eventually, she had written 17 books and had a tall pile of rejection letters from publishers and agents, who either didn't believe in her talents or didn't believe that there would be much interest in the genre. Finally, in 2010, frustrated by the publishers and agents who kept rejecting her, Amanda decided to see if she could sell her books on Amazon's Kindle. She self-published her vampire novel, *My Blood Approves,* on Amazon's site. She soon started selling nine books a week on the site. No great shakes, of course, but at least there was some interest, enough interest to prompt her to self-publish three additional books in the series on the site. It wasn't long after posting those three additional books that the series took off. Word obviously got around and from April 2010 through March 2011, she sold over a million copies of nine different books and earned $2 million in sales for those books. At one point, she was selling an average of 9000 books a day. Her sales strategy was brilliant. She sold the first books in her series at only 99 cents in an attempt to get her readers hooked on the series. The subsequent books in the series then sold for $2.99. Some of the conventional publishing houses scoffed at the idea of selling a book for only 99 cents, but Amanda Hocking sold such a huge volume of books that her sales soon put those criticisms to rest. Amanda Hocking is a poster child for the potential of self-publishing.

Now that we have some of the general information and some success stories out of the way, let's get into the nitty-gritty of how to write and publish a book.

How to Write A Book. Your Road Toward Making Big Bucks in Self-Publishing

Find a topic. Before you can write a book, you are going to have to select a subject or a topic. I suggest that you start out with a project that you are interested in. If you can find a topic or niche in which you are interested or passionate, you'll find that you'll enjoy writing the book a lot more. You'll also find that writing a book about something you are knowledgeable or interested in will require a lot less research.

If you don't have a particular subject or niche in mind and just want to write a book to earn extra income, I suggest that you first examine your personal areas of expertise or interest. For example, I have a friend of mine who is an avid biker (bicycle, not motorcycle). A few years ago, he was telling me how he had ridden on every bike trail in the state of Minnesota. He was telling me which trails he really enjoyed, and which trails he only mildly enjoyed. He even told me all about the ice cream shops or the coffee cafes that he would stop in as he traversed these trails. Many of the trails went through small towns that had interesting things to see or hidden gems, such as antique shops, diners, bakeries, or candy shops.

As he was relaying all of this information to me, I finally said, "You know, you should write a book about that. You're a fountain of information on Minnesota bike trails and I think people would be willing to pay for that information." He was taken aback by my idea and brushed it off by saying, "I could never do that. I'm not an author."

I didn't let the subject die and offered to help him self-publish his book if he was willing to gather all of the information. And I'm happy to say that he did publish a book on Minnesota bike trails. Although this book hasn't made him a millionaire, he enjoyed doing it, he is proud that he did it, and he now receives monthly royalty checks from the sales of his book. As a matter of fact, he now uses his bike book sales to fuel his weekend bike trips.

So the moral of the story for those of you who want to write books to earn some extra income: I suggest that you start with an area in which you are knowledgeable or passionate and then determine how to convey that information in a book. I have a friend who has coached youth sports for much of his adult life. He is also the parent of two boys who love sports. He has written a book for adults on how to coach their kids. Another friend of mine has been a midwife for over 20 years. She wrote a book targeted at expectant mothers. She discussed the benefits of using a midwife and discussed whether expecting parents should use a midwife or a doctor. Both the parent–coach and the midwife conveyed valuable information in their books and they've derived monthly supplementary income from the sales of those books.

In determining a topic for your book or books, don't be discouraged if there are already multiple books available on the subject you're considering. This might be a plus instead of a minus. For example, if you want to write a book on nutrition, you'll quickly note that you'll not be the first person to do so. There are thousands of books out there on nutrition. This should not discourage you, as it shows that there is definitely an interest in the subject. If you can bring a unique perspective to any topic, you'll have a chance to be successful in selling your book.

Develop a Working Title. Jot down ideas for the title of your book as you come up with them. This so-called title will simply be a working title, and you'll be able to change it any time before the book is published. But your working title will serve as a constant reminder of the topic of your book. If you are writing a self-help book, you will certainly want to come up with a title that will entice the reader to buy and read the book. Titles like "How to Lose 10 Pounds in 10 Days" and "How to Train Your New Puppy" will allow prospective buyers and readers to immediately determine if they have further interest in your book.

Develop an Outline. In writing a book, it's going to be important for you to establish some sort of organization with the content of that book. With this in mind, you'll need to develop an outline for the content of that book, possibly even a chapter by chapter outline which you can adhere to in writing the book.

Select a Template for Your Book. Many novice authors find it easier to use a template in writing their books. There are multiple sites on the internet that offer free book templates, including hubspot.com. In some instances, you'll have a number of different templates you can choose from. These templates will help you stay organized throughout the process of writing your book. As you become more accomplished or experienced at writing books, you probably won't need a template. However, it is a valuable tool for beginners.

Write the Book. After you've done all of the above, it's time to get into the nitty-gritty of writing the book itself. This, along with any research which might be required, will probably be the most time-consuming element in making a book. Most experienced authors will set a designated time to write their books, e.g., 2 hours a day, 15 hours a week, etc. They'll also determine which time of the day is best for them to do their writing, e.g., early morning, late evening after the kids have gone to bed, etc.

What if you're not a good writer or what if you have valuable information or a great story to impart to others but don't know how to put it on paper? If this is the case, you're probably going to have to hire someone to write your book for you. Ghostwriters are available on many sites, including Upwork.com. If you're going to hire a freelancer to write your book or your story, I encourage you to remember that they are only going to be able to be as good as the information you provide them with. I've ghostwritten many books and have gathered the information in a number of ways, including a written outline from the person who wants the book written, a collection of blogs by the same person, a weekly one- or two-hour tape-recorded phone interview or Skype interview, etc. Either way, you will have to figure out how to get the necessary information to the freelancer. If you are hiring a freelancer you haven't worked with before, I encourage you to request samples of their writing so you can review the quality and style of their writing and make sure it complies with your expectations. Along the same lines, in working with a freelancer, I suggest that you ask them to write the first chapter of your book for a nominal fee and then proceed with the remainder of the book after you've made sure you're on the right track. This sample chapter will benefit both you and the freelancer, as you'll want to make sure you're "on the same page" before you get too far into the project.

Adding Illustrations, Graphs, Photos. After you've written the book, you should determine whether the addition of illustrations, graphs, or photos will add value to the book. As an example, I just finished writing a book which tells the true story of a former US naval officer who was a Japanese prisoner-of-war in the Philippines in

World War II. Although the story itself was incredible, I knew that adding photos to the book would add to the value, as I knew that the readers would want to see the man whose story we told. And even though these were old black-and-white photos and weren't in mint condition, they added value to the book and we opted to include them. A friend of mine recently completed a pie recipe book. Obviously, photos of the pies add a lot to the value of the book, as people who buy recipe books are accustomed to photos of the recipe items. This friend had a limited budget in producing this recipe book, so she opted to take photos of the different pies with her cell phone instead of paying a professional photographer to do so.

Cover Design. Whether you're producing a printed book or an eBook, you should know that how you package that book is likely to be an extremely important factor in the sales of the book. If you've ever browsed books in a bookstore or in the library, you'll know that the cover or jacket of a book can certainly influence whether you buy that book or select that book to read. Packaging is very important. With this in mind, you'll want to create an attractive cover for your book. Unless you are a designer (most of us aren't), you're going to have to hire a freelancer to design your cover. Please know that there are many graphic artists who specialize in designing book covers. I have previously used the fiverr.com site to hire freelancers for my cover designs. I have always been able to hire someone for under $100 to do that and I've been able to get some great designs. Again, with these freelancers, their success may well depend on the instructions you give them. On the Fiverr site, you'll have many freelancers to choose from. In working with them, you have to tell them the size of the book you are looking to produce, whether you want a cover designed for a print book or an eBook or both, and you'll also have to provide the copy that you want on the cover of the book, including the title and a brief description of the book.

In working with freelancers to design covers, I have almost always opted to give them a photo or illustration which I want them to use on the cover. There are a number of stock photo sites on the internet which offer huge selections and excellent search engines for you to find photos or illustrations that you can use on your book covers. I have previously used istockphoto.com for my photo and illustration needs. On this site, I have generally been able to purchase a photograph for under $35 to use on my book covers. These are non-licensed photographs in which the photographers or illustrators post photos or illustrations on the site which are available for purchase on an on-going basis. The photographers or illustrators than get a cut every time a customer purchases their photo or illustration.

Formatting. Whether you want a printed book, an eBook, or both, your book is going to have to be formatted so it can be properly uploaded to the sites that will print or sell your book. If you have the time, you can certainly learn how to do the formatting yourself through tutorials on the internet. If you don't have the time (most people don't), you can always hire a freelancer to do that for you. Again, fiverr.com offers a wide selection of freelancers who will format your book for prices advertised from $15 to $100. In hiring a freelancer to format your book, you'll again need to give them the size of the book if you're going to have a printed book. You're also going to have to tell them who you plan to use to print or sell your books. In working with freelancers on some sites like the Fiverr site, please remember that these freelancers are from all over the world and there may be time differences or language differences involved. With many of these freelancers, English is a second language, but most of them are quite proficient in English. And most of them have done numerous formatting or cover design projects, so they're likely to know exactly what you will need to submit to various self-publishing platforms.

ISBN. If you're going to have a printed book, you'll need an ISBN. ISBN stands for International Standard Book Number and it is a 13-digit number used by publishers, booksellers, and libraries to identify books. ISBN numbers are not required for eBooks. Purchasing an ISBN is a simple process and there are a number of ISBN sellers on the internet. I use isbnservices.com and paid $18.99 for my most recent ISBN. That ISBN includes a barcode which can be used for scanning by booksellers and libraries.

Determining Your Sell Price. As a self-published author, you can set your own selling price. (If you were using a traditional publisher, they would dictate what price you sell at.) In determining a selling price, I always instruct authors to get on publishing platforms such as Amazon to find out what the books in their genre are selling for. Once you have determined that, you should settle on a selling price which falls somewhere within that range. If you are offering a printed version of the book, your sell price should be printed on the back cover of your book inside the ISBN and bar code area. In determining a price for a printed book, please remember that you should select the highest possible price you would sell the book at and then note that you will be able to discount that book when and if you see fit to do so. For example, I wrote a 250-page memoir for which I decided the maximum sell price would be $16. I set this price not only because it was comparable to the prices of other memoirs, but because I wanted my readers who ordered a printed copy from Amazon to be able to spend $20 or less, including shipping. I then made some personal appearances at book clubs and libraries and bookstores, and, in the case of book clubs and libraries, I was able to discount the book to $12 or $14 if they purchased on the spot. This was attractive to prospective readers as everyone likes a discount and they wouldn't have to pay for shipping as they would if they ordered from an internet source. At the time I was doing that (a few years ago), I was paying somewhere between $3 and $4 per book and buying about 25 to 50 books at a time for my presentations, so you can see that my profit margin was still very good, even when I discounted the book.

Pricing for eBooks is slightly different and prices are usually substantially less because there are no actual printing or materials involved. Most eBooks will sell anywhere from $2.99 to $9.99. If you use the Amazon Kindle Direct Publishing (KDP) platform to sell your book, you can expect royalties of 70% on any books that are sold within that $2.99-$9.99 price range. Anything that falls outside that price range, higher or lower, your royalties will drop to 35%. As you can see by those numbers, Amazon strongly prefers that you sell your eBooks on their platform for $2.99-$9.99. And eBooks are different than printed books in that you can't discount them whenever you see fit. For the most part, the selling price you establish is the price you'll sell the book. That said, you should note that KDP offers prospective readers the opportunity to sample a free chapter to see if they want to buy the book. They also offer a giveaway program in which you can offer your book for free when the book is first posted for sale, in an attempt to create interest for the book. Many authors have used this free offer to successfully promote their book and create subsequent sales from the interest they create.

In determining your price for eBooks, the genre of the book will be very important in determining the price. For example, if it is a romance book for which you are hoping for mass consumption, then you'll note that most of these romance novels are sold at the lower end of the price spectrum. On the other hand, if you have a historical non-fiction book such as the book I mentioned concerning the US naval officer who was a Japanese prisoner-of-war, you can probably get more money for that book, as it is a non-fiction account that is not targeted for mass consumption and will appeal mostly to war veterans and history buffs.

Upload Your Book. Now things start to get exciting. You're ready to roll. Your book is finished and it's time to upload it to the platform or platforms on which you intend to sell it. There are many platforms available for you to use in selling your book. I will outline a few of them here for your convenience, but please remember that there are additional options available to you.

1)   Amazon/Kindle. This is the most well-known platform for selling self-published books. Over two-thirds of all eBook purchases are made through Amazon's Kindle Direct Publishing (KDP), the platform I mentioned in the section immediately preceding this one. If you're serious about selling your book as a passive income stream, Amazon's Kindle platform should be at or near the top of your list. One of the things that make the KDP platform so popular is that your prospective readers can get the Kindle app for their computer, tablet, or phone. This means that it will be easy for them to purchase and read your book. Amazon also has a partnership with Audible which will allow you to easily convert your book to an audio format and sell additional books. I'll go into further detail on audiobooks in the paragraphs that follow. So, one of the big advantages of using the Amazon platform to sell your book is that it is the most popular platform for buying and selling books. Also, it offers you the opportunity to publish digital, printed, and audio versions of your book all in one platform.

2) **Nook.** Barnes & Noble is a large book retailer and their e-reader device is called the Nook. The Nook is responsible for about a quarter of all e-readership so this is another platform that you should strongly consider for any book you want to sell. Royalties with the Nook platform are very similar to those of Amazon/Kindle. Nook royalties are 65% of the list price for any books sold between $2.99 and $9.99; 40% for books sold outside that range.

3) **iBooks.** Publishing your book on iBooks will allow you to sell your books in the Apple iBookstore. It means that your book can be made available to anyone that has an iPhone, and IPad, or a Mac, all Apple devices.

4) **Others.** I've outlined the three main platforms above, but you should know that there are also other platforms available for you to use in selling your book. Although I won't go into detail with those other options here, I would at least like to mention a few of them, so you can research yourself if you have further interest. Platforms such as Smashwords, Kobo, and Scribd are also very viable platforms on which to sell books. They might not offer the large numbers that the "big three" platforms do, but they still offer the opportunity for you to sell more books and make more money.

Marketing Your Book. Tips for Maximizing Your Book Profits

Marketing Your Book. Just because you've finished writing your book and posted it for sale on various platforms doesn't mean that you're done. Marketing your book is one of the most crucial factors in making money from your book. A number of years ago, a friend of mine hosted a New Year's Eve party for his friends and co-workers. He purchased large amounts of food and cold beverages for his party, presuming that it would be the party of the year. When the clock struck midnight and the new year rolled in, he asked me what I thought was the reason why only less than a dozen people at his party. "I'm not sure", I responded. "Did you tell people you were having the party?" My friend responded that he had been so busy making party plans that he hadn't had the chance to tell a lot of people about the party. As he himself said, "I thought the word would get around."

Well, the same goes for your book. Now that you've invested time and money to write your book, it's time to tell people that it's available. You can't expect people to buy your book if they don't even know it exists.

With this in mind, I have some tips for you to market your book and sell it. If you want to maximize the extra money you earn from your book, you'll need to market it. And if you can market it successfully, you might be able to reap financial benefits from it for quite some time.

Here are some simple and inexpensive ways you can market your book:

1) **Social Media.** Most of us already have a social media presence. Social media offers you a great opportunity to get the word out about your new book. Authors have used social media platforms

such as Facebook, Instagram, Twitter, Tumblr, Reddit, and Pinterest to promote their new books. In many instances, they would offer a free sample for readers in an effort to get them interested to buy the book. Also, please know that you should not just use these platforms once to promote your book. I've used those platforms multiple times, to announce that the book is available, to publish positive reviews I get on the book, to remind people that your book would make a great holiday gift, etc.

2) **Blogs, Websites.** Do you have a blog or a website which you can use to direct visitors to the platforms where they can purchase your book? If so, you should make sure you use these platforms to promote your book. If not, you may want to consider creating a blog to promote your new book and any future books.

3) **Emails, Texts.** I have also used mass emails and texts to announce the availability of my books. Over the years, I've accumulated a substantial address book. All of these people are potential customers. So, whenever I have a new book available, I send a mass email to my contacts, including a sales flyer which shows the cover of the book along with a brief description of the book and where they can purchase the book.

4) **Bookmarks, Postcards.** Also, each time I have a new book out, I print some bookmarks and postcards which I can hand out to people that I meet in person. I don't actually mail many of the postcards, but I like to hand them out to people I meet. I like the size of postcards because they can contain more information than the smaller bookmarks. Bookmarks and postcards are inexpensive ways to promote your book. I think I paid $25 plus shipping for 500 bookmarks and $30 plus shipping for 500 postcards from an online source. I use these items almost like business cards, handing them out readily to just about everyone I meet.

Tips for Publishing Audio Books

The audiobook market is yet another platform for you to use in enhancing your self-published book sales. Although the audiobook market isn't as large as the printed book or eBook market, it is a burgeoning market that merits your consideration. In a day and age where podcasts and radio apps are popular, it is important to note that some people prefer to view or listen to things instead of reading them. Whether they are driving in a car, working out at the health club, or lying on the beach, some people like to listen to audiobooks. And, of course, there are other people who just don't like to read and they prefer audio or visual methods.

I'm of the belief that you should wait to see how successful your printed books or eBooks are before you decide to publish them as audiobooks. The reason I say this is because of the extra time and extra expense involved. Before you invest more time or money in your book, you should first determine if it is successful in printed or eBook format. If so, you should definitely publish your book in audio format. If you don't, you'll be leaving money on the table that you could be earning by using an audio format.

Audiobook Creation Exchange (ACX) is the most popular platform for audiobooks. If you add your audiobook to ACX, it will be available for sale on Amazon, Audible, and the Apple Audio Store. For those of you not familiar with Audible, it is a seller and producer of spoken audio entertainment, information, and educational programming on the internet. It is a top seller of digital audiobooks.

If you publish your book on ACX, you'll earn royalties of 20% to 40% of whatever your sell price is.

Here is some quick general information regarding converting your book from a printed or digital format to an audio format.

1) **Prepare Your Book for Audio.** You'll need to edit your printed or digital books so they can be used as audiobooks. In other words, remove everything that won't make sense in an audio format, i.e., no references to illustrations, photos, or graphs; no hyperlinks or "click here" prompts.

2) **Decide Who Will Record Your Audio.** If you're going to have an audiobook, you're going to have to determine who will record your book? Will you want to hire a narrator or will you want to record the book in your own voice? If you have an education book or a memoir, you'll be more likely to be the narrator for your own book than you would for a book of fiction in which you may be better served to use someone with an acting skillset. In my own experience, I have always hired a narrator, even for my own memoir. I've done that for a number of reasons, but mostly because I don't have a great narrator's voice. My throat gets dry very quickly when I talk a lot, and I'm sure that it would take me long periods of time to narrate a book so listeners would quickly tire of my raspy voice. Also, I have a relatively noisy home environment, including a lot of street noise, and I am afraid the background noise would be too distracting to the listener. I had thought previously about renting a recording studio to record my book, but I feel that the money I would have spent renting a studio could just as well be spent in paying a narrator.

3) **Hiring a Narrator.** Hiring a narrator may not be as expensive as you might think. I have an associate who hires narrators on a frequent basis and he is usually able to hire someone for less than $500. He tells me that there are two sites he would recommend in hiring a freelance narrator. Those sites are Upwork and Voices. ACX also has narrators you can hire for your book. In hiring any freelance narrator, you should absolutely ask them to provide previous samples of their work. And, you might also ask them to narrate a small portion of your book before you officially hire them. In this way, you can make sure they are a good fit for your project before you get too far into the book.

4) **Rent a Recording Studio; Narrate Your Own Book.** If you want to narrate your own book, and if your home or office environment is too noisy to do so, you may have to rent a recording studio to use in narrating your book. I have a friend who tells me that this can be a 10- to 20-hour process, depending on the length of your book, so you may have to book the studio for multiple days. Again, beware that using your voice for such a long period of time may affect the quality of your voice, so you might have to rent the studio in smaller blocks of maybe three or four hours at a time.

If you want to learn more about creating an audiobook, I suggest that you visit selfpublishingschool.com, where Chandler Bolt has an extensive article on exactly how to publish an audiobook.

Six Steps Toward Earning Extra Income by Publishing Online Courses

I'd be remiss if I did not discuss how publishing online courses can create additional revenue streams for you. The market for online courses and online learning is getting bigger and bigger. The research firm Global Market Insights projects that online learning courses could reach $240 billion by 2023. That's an astronomical number.

With this in mind, I encourage you to consider developing online courses to create additional passive income streams for yourself. Here are some simple tips to get you started on developing an online course or courses:

1) **Find a topic.** What are you an expert at? Do you have information that is valuable to others…to the point that others will be willing to pay to learn that information? Or, even if you are not an expert, can you become an expert? One of the major success stories in online courses is that of Purna Duggirala, a man from India who goes by the name of Chandoo. A number of years ago, Chandoo recognized an opportunity to make money by hosting online courses. He noticed that people did not properly know how to use the Excel software program, so he came up with a series of courses in which he taught subscribers how to become excellent or awesome at Excel. He made over $1 million in 2014 with that concept. Again, we all know that these success stories only show the top range a person can earn. It's unlikely that you'll earn that kind of cash with your online courses. But again, there's no harm in dreaming. Even if you can garner an additional $500 to $1000 every month from your online course or courses, I'm sure you'd take it.

In determining a topic for your online courses, I suggest that you first take a personal inventory of your own knowledge to see if there is anything you can impart to people who would be willing to pay for your expertise. Are you an expert at technology? Can you teach coding or programming? Do you speak multiple languages? Can you teach one of those languages to people who are planning to visit a foreign country? A friend of mine is originally from the Philippines. Besides now speaking impeccable English, she speaks fluent Visayan and Tagalog, two languages that are spoken by many Filipinos. So, with the ability to speak these languages, she created an online mini-course series in which she teaches English-speaking people who are getting ready to visit the Philippines how to speak those native languages. She has been quite successful in getting people to subscribe to her courses and has derived a nice supplemental income from those courses.

If you don't have any areas where you would consider yourself an expert, you can always become an expert simply by garnering the information you have a passion for and then inserting that information into a course that is available online to others. I read a story about a man who knew nothing about coding, but by the time he finished reading multiple books on the subject, taking some online courses and tutorials, he knew more than almost all of the people who were interested in the same subject. So even though he hadn't started out as an expert, he became an expert with valuable information that people were willing to pay for.

2) **Create a course outline.** If you're going to create an online course, you'll most certainly need an outline for that course. You'll not only use that outline in conveying information to subscribers, but you'll also use that outline to sell the course to prospective subscribers, who are sure to want to know what the course entails before they enroll in it. In setting up your course, please know that most online courses are limited to a maximum of 20 minutes per session. After that, subscribers start to lose interest. I strongly suggest that you set up a series of 15- to 20-minute courses that can teach people everything they want to know about whatever subject you're teaching. That might entail as few as three-course sessions or as many as 10. Either way, limit your sessions to 20 minutes. And remember, each course should get your subscribers closer to the goals and objectives of your course.

3)   **Determine the price of your course.** In determining a price for your online course, please know that the length of the course should not be the main determinant. First, you should check to see what your competitors in the same subject are selling their courses for. Then, you should look at how your expertise falls within the spectrum of those people who are offering similar courses. For example, if Bill Gates or Paul Allen were to offer a course on how to use Windows, it's safe to assume that you're probably not going to be able to charge the same amount for a similar course. I say that somewhat tongue-in-cheek, but if you're a neophyte in the field for which your offering an online course, you're probably not going to be able to charge as much as an expert in the field. Finally, in determining the price for your online course, you should consider how much value you are giving the course subscriber. For example, if you're going to offer an online course which can be used to make thousands of dollars, you should be able to charge a lot more for that course than you would in offering to teach Portuguese to people who are planning on visiting Brazil. Or if your online course is solving a problem, a course that solves a major problem should obviously be priced higher than a course that solves a minor problem. Use common sense to set your sell price, and don't be afraid to test different price points. It's your course and you should be able to set whatever price you like for that course, as long as people are willing to subscribe.

I'd like to mention one other thing in regards to pricing for online courses. Yes, you'll be able to make money if you can <u>tell</u> people how to do something, but you'll be able to make even more money if you can <u>show</u> them how to do something. And finally, you'll be able to charge even more if you can offer support for the information you are trying to teach. For example, if you have a course on how to self-publish a book, are you available to answer individual questions your subscribers might have.

4) **Create the course content.** Using your course outline, you should create course content for each of your lesson segments. Depending on your own personal preference, you can decide whether you'll want to work from a script or not, but you'll definitely want to work from an outline. Many of the most successful online courses do not work from a script and are more casual and conversational, but almost all of them work from an outline.

5) **Create the course.** Your next step is to create the course itself. By now, you'll have decided if your course is going to be a written course, an audio course, or a video course. Obviously, video courses are the most successful, because people like to see visuals as they learn. If you're going to do a video course, you won't need to hire a video expert to shoot or edit your lessons. You should be able to do this on your phone, and you should know that there are many easy-to-use tools and software programs available. Programs such as Camtasia and Quicktime are among the programs that can be used for screen recordings.

When you are creating your course, you should remind yourself that it's not realistic to expect your lesson video recording to have the feel of a major television production. The content of the lesson will be more important than the presentation and you will certainly get better at the production of your lessons as you become more experienced at doing so.

6) **Launch your course.** There are a ton of different platforms available to host your online courses. Instead of trying to go through a multitude of these platforms, I will tell you how one of the most popular platforms works so you can get an idea of what you might expect in publishing and selling the online courses you develop. Udemy.com is the world's largest online learning platform. More than 30 million students have taken courses on Udemy; over 50,000 instructors offer over 130,000 courses in over 60 languages. This will give you an idea of the scope of the Udemy platform. Anyone can post a course on Udemy. If you want to charge a fee to the students on Udemy, you will need to complete a free application which is usually approved within two days. For any students you get to take your course, you will receive 97% of the course fee. Udemy will take a 3% commission. If Udemy secures students for your courses via their own marketing, they will then take a 50% commission amount and the instructor will receive the other 50%. As Udemy does not charge a hosting fee, the only way they make money is by selling courses. Udemy is widely known as a good place to start for the novice online instructors, as it offers a simple way for instructors/sellers to assemble content like PowerPoint slides, PDF documents, and YouTube videos into a coherent course. The Udemy platform also offers a variety of marketing tools to help sellers sell their course.

Other popular online learning course platforms include Teachable, WizIQ, Thinkific, and Ruzuka. If you want to take a more in-depth look at the different online course platforms which are available, I recommend that you visit www.learningrevolution.net/sell-online-courses/, where they have a nice article outlining 15 of the best online learning course platforms.

Whether you're publishing printed books, digital books, audiobooks, or online learning courses, these self-publishing methods offer you some excellent opportunities to create passive income streams which can make you money for long periods of time after you've done the initial work to develop the materials. These self-publishing venues are not 100% passive income, as there is some initial work required. However, once you have published the materials, you should be able to derive additional income for long periods of time—weeks, months, even years—with very little additional work.

Chapter 3--Blogging for Big Profits

Another great way for you to create additional passive income will be for you to create a series of blogs. We're all familiar with the multitude of blogs that appear on the internet, but you may not understand exactly how bloggers make income from their blogs. With this chapter, I will provide some tips on how you can start a successful blog that can provide you with additional income. Like most passive income streams, starting a blog will require some time and effort. But once you are set up, your blogs can continue to provide income for months, weeks, and even years.

The Truth About Earning Through Blogs

I'm sure you're aware that there are millions of blogs on the internet. Anyone who has used Google or Bing can attest to the fact that there is a blog on the internet for just about every topic imaginable. Some of those blogs make money; some of them don't. Some of those blogs are intended to make money; others are not. Some of the blogs intended to make money do not make money. With this chapter, we will concentrate on blogs that are intended to make money and I will give you some tips and techniques as to how to create a blog and then how to monetize that blog.

Determine a Niche. In starting a blog that is going to provide you with additional income, you will first have to find a niche for that blog. A niche is a particular market segment or audience. Unless your blog has a specific niche or target audience, it's going to be very difficult for you to monetize it. Yes, there are bloggers on the internet who write about random topics or about anything and everything. But most of those bloggers don't make money from their blogs. Bloggers who make money from their blogs usually have specific topics or niches that they use to attract visitors to their site or solve specific problems.

In determining a niche for your blog, you should remember that most people visit blogs to gather information or to solve a specific problem. If you can provide them with the information they are looking for in an attractive package, then you'll have a chance to have a successful blog. It's important to note that whatever niche you choose, there are probably already existing blogs that already fall within that niche. Don't let this discourage you. If you can convey valuable information and you can convey it in a straightforward, entertaining, and attractive manner, you'll have a chance to be successful with your blog.

Here are examples of some of the most popular blog niches:

--How to Make Money.

--Health & Fitness.

--Lifestyle.

--Food.

--Personal Finance.

--Beauty and Fashion.

In choosing a niche for your blog, I strongly suggest that you select a topic or an area that you are passionate about. If you are passionate about something, you'll be much more likely to be able to write blogs about that subject. Your readers will be able to sense your passion and you'll be a lot less likely to abandon your blog or blog series because you've become bored with it or lost interest in it.

I'll give you an example. I have a close friend who is an avid baseball fan. His favorite team is the Minnesota Twins professional baseball team. My friend, who when I first met him was working a regular day job, is such a baseball fan that he spends almost all of his spare time thinking and talking about baseball. He lives and breathes baseball. One day, it dawned on him that he might be able to make money from his favorite hobby. So, he started a Minnesota Twins baseball blog in which he posted articles he wrote about his favorite team. He found quickly that there were many other Minnesota Twins fans who were desperate to read about their team every day and they wanted a daily dose of information about the Twins, even during the off-season. So, what started as a weekly blog, quickly became a daily blog or post. He now has a stable of regular contributors who contribute to his Minnesota Twins-themed website. He has a forum in which his site visitors or blog readers can comment on various subjects involving the Twins. The site now has semi-monthly podcasts in which he and some of his associates discuss the Twins. He is a guest on radio shows and talks about the Twins. Bottom line, he has turned his passion and his modest initial blogs into a full-time job. He is truly doing what he loves. His Twins website/blog spot now gets so many daily visitors that he is easily able to sell site advertising to companies that are looking to reach the same niche audience. Those advertisers include ticket brokers, bars and restaurants that are near the Twins stadium, travel agencies that coordinate spring training vacations to watch the Twins, etc. It's amazing to think that all of this started with one paltry blog and has blossomed into a full-scale profitable business.

In reviewing this example, it is important to remember that my friend selected a niche he was passionate about, one he was not going to lose interest in. He was going to think and talk baseball whether he had a blog or not. But in launching his blog, he quickly discovered that many people have the same passion he has, and he was able to monetize that passion into a profitable business.

If you want to determine a possible niche for your blog and you're not quite sure what a good niche would be for you, let me suggest that you ask yourself the following questions: What is your favorite hobby? How do you spend most of your free time? Is there a subject or topic that you could go on and on about if someone is willing to listen? What were your favorite subjects in high school or college? What things do you like to read about, learn about, or gather information on? If you were independently wealthy and you did not have to work for a living, what activities or pastimes would you choose to fill your time?

Write Some Blogs. Once you have determined your niche, you can start writing blogs. Instead of writing just one blog, I suggest that you write a series of blogs so you can post them on a regular basis (weekly, monthly, etc.). Prepare some kind of an outline in which you determine and detail the topics for each of your blogs. Some bloggers prefer to place all their content online at the same time and then leave it at that. For example, if the niche is targeted at bloggers and is How to Start and Make Money from a Blog, the blogger could post a number of blogs all at the same time. Topics for the individual blogs could include how to choose a blog niche, how to write a blog, how to choose a blog platform, ways to make money from your blog, etc. Each different topic could have a separate blog and, in reality, you could post all of these blogs at the same time and be done with the writing. On the other hand, if your niche requires or benefits from frequent updating, you'll want to write additional blogs as new information becomes available. For example, with the Minnesota Twins blog site I described, the Twins play 162 games in a regular season and it's reasonable to think that any blogs concerning the team will require at least weekly blogs. This particular site has become so successful that it now features new blogs on a daily basis. It's important to note that these blogs are not all written by the founder of the blog site. He now has a stable of writers who contribute blogs to the site on a regular basis.

What if you're not a writer? Can you still have a blog? Yes, you can. You can hire a freelancer to write your blogs. There are a number of freelancing sites you can use to hire a writer, including Upwork and Fiverr. If you want to convey specific information in your blogs, then you will obviously have to relay this information to the freelance writer. But I know other people who simply give the freelancer a topic and then the freelancer will research the topic and write the article. In hiring a freelancer, you should try to find someone that fits your style and someone you can work with on an on-going basis. You may have to go through a freelancer or two before you can find a freelancer that suits your needs. Depending on the length of your blogs, you should be able to find a freelancer that can write a blog for you at about $25 to $40 per blog. If research is required on the part of the freelancer, you can expect to pay more.

Select Your Platform. There are a lot of different platforms available for you to publish your blog. Some of them are free; others charge a nominal monthly fee to host your blogs. In this section, I'll detail a few of the options available to you and then you can research these options further as you decide which platform you should use.

1) **WordPress** is the most popular blogging platform. It is especially popular with beginner bloggers as it is free, it doesn't require a lot of technical expertise such as coding or design, and it has lots of different themes to choose from. Please know that WordPress might not have the functionality you are looking for unless you pay for their upgrades. However, as a beginner, you can decide which "bells and whistles" you want to upgrade to later to make your site look more professional, to have access to more themes, designs, and plug-ins, etc. For example, WordPress.org charges about $3 a month for hosting and offers more than 1500 free themes and 20,000 free plug-in options. Again, if you are a beginner, I suggest that you start with the free package and see if that fits your needs. If not, you will be able to upgrade at any time.

2) **Blogger** is a platform owned by Google. It's also free and offers free access to Google tools such as AdSense and Analytics. It is an easy platform to use and it's a great platform for beginner bloggers.

3) **Tumblr** is another free platform that is a social media site. It's great for microbloggers, people who want to post many short notes frequently.

4) **Typepad** and **WIX** are pay-per-month business platforms that charge nominal monthly hosting fees of less than $10 per month. Those platforms are geared toward business blogs. They are easy to use. WIX has ecommerce functions that make it attractive to small businesses. Unlike WordPress, Blogger, and Tumblr, both Typepad and Wix allow you to have your own domain name. For example, your domain name will always have wordpress (Wordpress) or blogspot (Blogger) in the title. This may not matter to you, but if you are a business, that might be an important consideration and you may want instead use a third party server such as BlueHost or HostGator to host

your site. Both of those third-party servers offer very reasonable pricing for hosting at less than $3 a month.

Promote Your Blog. Common sense tells us that no one is going to read your blog unless they know it exists. Some bloggers are reluctant to "toot their own horn" and tell others that they have a blog. Don't be shy about this. When you publish your first blog, use email blasts and social media to tell people you know about your new blog and tell them how they can access it. If you don't do this, then you may find that your mother is the only person reading it.

Use Your Blog to Expand Other Related Passive Income Activities. If you're smart, you will tie your blogs into your other passive income activities. Not only will this help produce additional income, it should also help you create a loyal following. Many people use their blogs to promote their newsletters. They will instruct readers to sign up for monthly or quarterly newsletters. Along the same lines, bloggers will direct their readers to the podcasts or the videos they have produced. I know quite a number of bloggers who have accumulated the blogs they've written over the years and compiled those blogs into eBooks. It's all interrelated. You should plan to have multiple venues to promote your passive income activities.

Seven Ways to Earn Income from Blogging

There are multiple ways you can make money from blogging. No, it's not an overnight process and there is some initial work required. However, once you're up and running, you could be able to supplement your income substantially by blogging. I've selected seven of my favorite ways for you to make money blogging. Here they are:

1) **Cost-per-click (CPC) advertising.** With this concept, advertisers will pay each time a visitor to your site clicks on one of the ads on your site. It's a "finder's fee" of sorts. CPC advertising can include full-color ads which appear on your site; it can also include simple text advertising in your blog. For example, if you have a baseball blog in which the topic is "Different ways to get tickets to the big game" and one of the options is to buy tickets from an authorized ticket broker, you would be able to mention the name of that ticket broker in your text, and, provided that the ticket broker is a participating advertiser, you'll be able to earn a small sum every time someone clicks on that ad and the ad takes them to the advertiser's site. I should mention up front that you're not going to get rich from CPC advertising until the numbers of people visiting your site reach respectable numbers. Companies that offer easy to implement CPC internet advertising include Google's AdSense, infolinks, media.net, and Chitika. If you have further interest in CPC advertising, I suggest that you visit some of these aforementioned sites to learn more about what advertising programs are available to you as a blogger.

2) **Sell your own advertising on your blog.** If you want, you can take it upon yourself to go "old school" and sell ads on your site. You can arrange yourself for advertisers on your site or you can have a third-party seller do that for you. To give you an example of a sell-your-own advertising approach, if you have a blog regarding a specific bike trail, you could certainly approach a bike rental place along that trail or a restaurant at one of the stops along the trail and see if they want to advertise on your blog. Nothing wrong with selling ads to your blog the old-fashioned way…and you will be able to keep 100% of the ad revenue yourself. If you don't want to bother with selling ads on your site, you can register with a third-party seller and they can do that for you. Companies like BuySellAds or BlogAds are third-party

advertising sellers who will sell ads for your blog. They'll then give you 70 to 75% of the ad sales and then keep the remaining amounts in return for their efforts. Please note that third-party sellers are not interested in low-traffic blogs, so you'll have to get your traffic to a decent level before you can even consider using a third-party seller.

3)   **Sell text links on your blog.** I mentioned text link advertising in the above section on CPC advertising. There is a company called LinkWorth that specializes in this kind of text advertising. With LinkWorth, you'll be able to link a piece of text in your blog to a page on another site. Every time one of your blog readers clicks on this link, you'll receive a commission from Linkworth. This is another program that requires a decent amount of traffic to your blog before you can begin working with LinkWorth, so if you're a new blogger and your blog traffic is still minimal, you'll have to get your traffic up before you can begin doing these cost-per-click text links.

4)   **Online courses and workshops.** In the previous chapter, I told you how you could make money by self-publishing online courses and workshops. Any blog you do should link to any related online courses and workshops that you've produced. Again, all of these things are interrelated and you should never miss an opportunity to advertise one medium on another medium.

5)   **Books and eBooks.** Just as you'll want to use your blog to promote your online courses and workshops, you'll want to use it to promote any printed books, digital books, or audiobooks which you have produced.

6) **Speaking gigs.** Once your blog traffic has reached a reputable level, you will be able to advertise yourself as an expert on whatever subject your blog covers. This may bring speaking opportunities in which you can enhance your passive income. I had a recent speaking engagement which resulted from my blogs concerning the history of the small town I was born in. My audience was the town historical society and, although I didn't get paid for my speaking engagement, I was able to sell 71 of my printed books after my presentation. The presentation was well worth my time financially, as I made over $10 per printed book for a 90-minute presentation which I enjoyed immensely. So, if you're not yet someone who can command a fee of $10,000 to $100,000 per speech, don't worry about it. You can still achieve profits on a lower scale by using your blog to promote your products and services.

7) **Affiliate marketing.** Affiliate marketing involves recommending or referring the products and services of other companies and their products and services in return for a commission. Are you recommending other products or services on your blog? Or could you recommend other products or services on your blog? If you do or if you can, then I suggest that you consider affiliate marketing to earn some passive income. Again, the money you can earn will be directly related to the number of people who read your blogs, however when your blog traffic reaches a respectable level, then it's time for you to start exploring affiliate marketing opportunities. There are a ton of affiliate programs available to you. I've listed some of the most popular programs for you to use as a starting point when your blog is at a level where you can start to reap the benefits of affiliate marketing. (I've provided additional information about affiliate marketing in the chapter that follows.)

--Amazon Associates

--eBay Partner Network

--BlueHost

--HostGator

--HostPapa

--DreamHost

--AliExpress

As I've detailed in this chapter, you will be able to earn passive income from your blog. Obviously, before you can do that, you'll have to get your blog up and running and get the traffic levels for that blog to a point where you can earn some extra cash from it. But once you've done that, you can start reaping the benefits from it.

Chapter 4—Make Passive Income on the Internet Now

Most of us have heard the term "make money while you are sleeping". Affiliate marketing is the passive income activity which is most often associated with the concept of making money while you are sleeping. In this chapter, I'll outline how you can make money with affiliate marketing and with dropshipping, another passive income activity which is often related to affiliate marketing. I'll tell you why you need to consider these activities for your passive income streams and I'll tell you how to get started.

All You Need to Know About Affiliate Marketing

Affiliate marketing is when you recommend or refer the products or services of other companies in return for a commission. With affiliate marketing, you are the affiliate. You search for products that you enjoy or would like to endorse and then promote that product through your various media, including websites, social media, written blogs or video blogs, and emails, and then you earn a portion of the profit when a sale is made for that product or service. Sales are tracked through affiliate links from one website to another.

I'll give you a quick example. A woman has a series of blogs or podcasts that are targeted at new parents. As a new parent herself, she has used a baby stroller which she really likes and would recommend to anyone. With these in mind, she writes one of her blogs or does one of her vlogs (video blogs) with this stroller brand as the main subject. She highly recommends the stroller based on her experience in using it and in her blog or vlog she provides a link to the site of the manufacturer, where customers can visit and subsequently purchase the stroller. For each stroller sold as a result of the woman's blog or vlog, the woman will receive a commission for her part in recommending the stroller and then telling the customer where they can purchase it.

As this book is being written, current statistics show that 81% of all brands and 84% of all companies are using affiliate marketing as a means to sell their products or services. Those percentages will continue to increase as companies continue to increase their affiliate marketing spending. In 2018, 16% of all internet sales resulted from affiliate marketing. That's an impressive number. Data now shows that companies selling products and services through affiliate marketing will spend 62% of what they would spend through traditional marketing efforts, so as these companies realize that they can spend less and be more successful in selling through affiliate marketing, they will begin to focus more of their sales efforts on that activity and affiliate marketing will continue to grow in future years.

From the consumer standpoint, consumers may or may not be aware that you will be earning a commission as a result of recommending a product or service. Either way, most of them won't care, as they will almost always end up paying the same price for the product. Your commission will be built into the retail price of the product and the consumer will not pay additional to cover your commissions.

As an affiliate, you can be paid for three different actions which direct the consumer to the seller. The most popular action will be Pay Per Sales. With this action, you direct the consumer to the seller and the consumer purchases the product. You can also get paid with a Pay for Lead action. Again, you direct the consumer to a seller site and the consumer then does any of a number of required actions, possibly completing a contact form, signing up for a product trial, subscribing to a newsletter, downloading software, etc. In these instances, the seller will value these actions enough to pay you a commission. Another form of affiliate marketing involves the affiliate being paid on a Pay Per Click basis. Usually, Pay Per Click involves the consumer clicking a link on your site to move to the seller's site. The seller values this enough to allocate a commission to the affiliate.

Why be an affiliate marketer? With affiliate marketing, you really can earn money while you are sleeping. Once you've invested an initial amount of time in promoting a product, you can continue to earn money for your efforts long after you recommended the seller's product or service. Once you have directed the consumer to the seller, you can step out of the transaction and don't have to spend any time in supporting the customer after the sale. Affiliate marketing is attractive to many people because it allows them to earn passive income from home without much initial investment and without having to create the product or service you're going to help sell. There are no affiliate fees to worry about and you can get started quickly without a lot of time or effort.

Five Steps Toward Becoming an Affiliate Marketer

How can you get started on your journey to becoming an affiliate marketer? Here are some simple steps you can take to become an affiliate marketer. By the time you complete these steps, you should be well on the road to becoming a successful affiliate marketer and earning passive income while you sleep.

1) **Find or determine a niche.** If you're going to get into affiliate marketing, you're going to have to determine a niche for that

marketing. In determining a niche or niches for your affiliate marketing, I strongly suggest that you find niches or areas that you are passionate about or strongly interested in.

I'll use myself and my wife as examples. In doing a personal inventory, I have a number of passions, many of which are my hobbies. I love baseball, especially Major League Baseball. I also love being a youth baseball coach. I also love reading and writing. I consider myself to be an expert on writing, ghostwriting, self-publishing, and editing. Finally, I love biking and I love dogs. My wife, on the other hand, loves to talk about parenting issues. She is a midwife by trade and is very knowledgeable about midwifery. She is a fashionista and is extremely knowledgeable and passionate about handbags, as our credit card statements attest.

In looking at your interests, you should now try to determine whether there is enough depth there for you to present yourself as an expert on the subject. Is there enough depth in the subject that you could write 25, 50, or 100 blogs about it? For my purposes, I could write a blog about baseball every day. On the other hand, even though I enjoy biking, I would find it difficult to write 25 to 50 blogs about biking.

If you have enough depth in the niche you are considering, the next thing to consider is whether you can make money in recommending products or services in that niche. With the interests of my wife and I, a couple of things pop out at me. Regarding my love for dogs, I am well aware that pet products and supplies are a huge industry. Even a smaller industry such as bicycling has a lot of different products available, including bikes, helmets, gloves, bike bags, water bottles, and bottle holders, bike tire repair kits, etc. Obviously, there is a market for women's handbags, thanks to my wife. On the other hand, it's my feeling that there isn't as much money to be made in the youth coaching, as there aren't many products required to coach a youth baseball team. Yes, uniforms, bats, and balls may be required, but most coaches already have sources for those products. Yes, there may be some online coaching workshops which may be available to sell or some books along the same lines, but the amount of products in this niche seems to be somewhat limited compared to the products available in the dog niche or even in the smaller biking niche. So, in taking an inventory of the things you're passionate about, you should determine if there is money to be made within those niches. If there aren't any or that many products to sell within that niche, then it's not a good affiliate marketing niche. No products mean no sales.

2) Are there affiliate marketing programs available within your niche? After you've settled on a niche that you're interested in, it's time for you to find out what's out there in terms of product and services you can promote with your websites, blogs, vlogs, and emails. For example, if I decide that I want to get into an affiliate marketing program regarding puppy training, I'd want to find out what products are out there that are related to puppy training or dog training. On a slightly broader scale, what products are out there that are related to puppies in general.

You'll have to spend some time researching this. But because the products and services you find will be the source of your income for this affiliate marketing endeavor, the time you spend will be well worth it. When you find these products or services, you should make sure they are of good quality. If you are marketing items of poor quality, it will surely damage your reputation or credibility. Many affiliate marketers will test products or services before recommending them. Also, you should make sure that the products you're recommending to consumers are products that you want to be associated with. It might behoove you to read the posted product reviews of any products or services you are considering for your affiliate marketing efforts.

As you find affiliate marketing programs within your niche, you should see if there are similar sellers to you within the niche. If so, that's probably a good indication, as other affiliates would probably not be recommending those sellers if they are not making money from it.

3) **Time to build a site.** Now that you've done your research, it's time for you to create a vehicle in which you can disseminate information to consumers. It's time to build a website. Although there are many different web hosts out there, many beginners use WordPress because it is easy to use and it's free (although upgrades are available). Building a website is much, much easier than ever before and you won't need to be a coder or a designer. No technical knowledge required.

In building a website, you have to first purchase a domain, which will be the address for your website. GoDaddy and NameCheap are both very popular sources from which you can purchase a domain name. The last time I looked, you could purchase domain names from both these companies at under $15 per year. In selecting your domain name, you should know that it's possible that the domain name you want is already in existence and you may have to come up with some other options.

After you have a domain name, you will have to find a host for your website. Again, GoDaddy is a popular option, as are BlueHost and HostGator, companies I previously mentioned. All three of those companies have plans that start under $3 a month. If you purchase your domain name and your web hosting from different companies, you will need to link the two together. However, this is a very easy process that is outlined on the abovementioned sites.

Now that you have purchased a domain name and selected a host for your website, it's time for you to install your content management system. (e.g., WordPress or whatever content management system you have chosen.) In the process of doing this, you'll have the chance to select a theme to use for your website. While most content management systems offer a large selection of themes to choose from, you should select a theme that works well with whatever niche you have chosen.

4) Create content for your website. Now that you have your domain name, your web host, and your theme, you can begin creating content for your website. Whatever content you create should certainly be related to the niche you have chosen. Your content should be interesting enough, engaging enough, or informative enough to keep your web visitors coming back. Here are some basic ideas on popular ways to convey content on affiliate marketing sites:

Reviews. Many affiliates will provide reviews of the products or services they are trying to sell. If possible, you will have used the products you're reviewing. This should help you immensely in reviewing the product. If you haven't used the product, many consumers may be able to sense that you haven't done so.

Blogs. Affiliates often use blogs to promote the items they are trying to sell. Although the blog doesn't necessarily need to be all about the item you're trying to sell, it should at least mention that product or service within the article in the appropriate place. Many blogs will address problems, questions, and then hopefully provide solutions or recommendations on how those problems can be solved. In working your affiliate marketing, you'll obviously want to recommend your affiliate products as possible solutions to the problems.

In-text Content Links. I'm sure you've visited websites and read articles which have links within the text of those articles. If you click on those links, they'll take you to other websites where you can view additional content or purchase products or services. These are called in-text context links and they provide a very effective means of affiliate marketing. By using in-text links, you'll be able to earn money if people from your site go immediately to these other sites and purchase products.

Informational Products. Many websites will offer free informational products to build their mailing lists. If you can build a substantial mailing list, you will be much more successful in your affiliate marketing. Affiliates will also offer free newsletters or free eBooks to consumers who register their names and email addresses.

Banner ads. Many affiliates use banner ads on their websites to direct people to their affiliate sites. These banner ads can be very effective, though you wouldn't want to clutter your site with so many ads that your content gets lost. You might also lose your credibility as an expert.

5) **Market your site, build your audience.** Now that you have your website up and running, it's important to let people know it exists. There are a number of ways you can build the audience for your website. In doing this, it is important for you to continue adding valuable content to your site, content that will keep people coming

back to your site. If someone is going to visit your site once and then never visit again, you're very unlikely to be successful in your affiliate marketing efforts. Here are ways you can build your following:

Social media. You're probably already participating in various social media venues. It's important for you to use those venues to promote your new website. Social media such as Facebook, Instagram, Twitter, and Pinterest offer opportunities for you to get the word out about your new site.

Expertise. If you are an expert in something (i.e.—puppy training), you should make yourself available to do guest posts on other related high-traffic blogs. Offer to write blogs to be posted on these other sites in return for them mentioning or providing a link to your web address. Guest posting on someone else's established site, you'll be able to get the word out about your website.

Search Engine Optimization (SEO). SEO will also be important in directing people to your website. If you're not very familiar with SEO, I suggest that you take some time to read a few articles on SEO and what you can do to optimize your website in internet searches. If you don't have the time to do this, you might consider hiring an SEO marketing expert to do this for you.

Paid advertising. Another option you can use to drive people to your website is paid advertising. Social media sites generally offer affordable ads. Or you can buy banner ads on small niche sites that are related to your niche. GoogleAdWords might also be a good option for you, depending on your niche.

Make Money Dropshipping

Dropshipping is yet another way for you to make passive income. For those of you who are not exactly sure what dropshipping is, let me provide a description that may help. Dropshipping is a retail fulfillment method in which you will be able to sell the retail products of your choice on an online store which you create. The benefit of dropshipping for you is that you will not need to open a brick-and-mortar store with its large overhead and monthly lease and insurance costs. You won't have to hire and pay employees or do payroll taxes. You won't have to carry or stock any merchandise. All of that will be handled by a third party, a supplier who will store and warehouse the items you're selling and who will ship the items you sell directly to the consumer.

You'll be responsible for securing sales for the items you are selling. You will also be able to set prices on these items, but those prices will have to be comparable to what the market dictates or offered by competitors or companies selling the same merchandise. It should be pointed out that with dropshipping programs, the products you are selling are likely to be sold by other companies as well, so your pricing will probably need to remain competitive and you might find that your profit margins will be slim, depending on the item.

Let me take you through how this process works behind the scenes. Let's say that I have an online store that sells custom minor league baseball jerseys. All of these jerseys contain the logos and designs of different minor league baseball teams. A customer purchases a jersey from my website for $40 and pays me online for that jersey. I then forward the order to my supplier or wholesaler, who is selling the jersey to me for $28. The supplier then sends the order to the customer using a shipping label with my name on it. This "blind label" is used so the customer will recognize the shipper of the item. It is also used so the customer will not be able to bypass me and go directly to the supplier or wholesaler. When the supplier or wholesaler ships the jersey to the customer, they will charge me for the $32 cost of the jersey plus shipping. So, my role in the entire sale is simple: I secured the sale and sent it to the supplier, and I sent an acknowledgment to the customer. The supplier made, stored, and shipped the jersey. I also collected a cool $8 for the sale. All in all, as an affiliate marketer, I am a middleman. As you can see, dropshipping is a simple business model that requires a minimal investment in time and money on your part. If you find the right niche and the right supplier, dropshipping can be a profitable venture.

Five Essential Steps in Creating Dropshipping Business

Here are five essential steps for achieving dropshipping success.

1) **Find a niche.** We've discussed how important it is to find a niche in the previous sections on blogging and affiliate marketing. The same principles apply here. If you're going to get involved in dropshipping, you'll be involved in a venue in which you're likely to have many competitors. With this in mind, the more you are able to refine your niche, the more successful you'll be. For example, if you want to fine-tune your niche, you can go from pet products down to dog products down to puppy products or dog training products, etc. You get the picture. The more you fine-tune your niche, the fewer your competitors and the higher your profit margins will be.

2) **Research your competition.** Speaking of competition, it will be important for you to research your competition to find out how much they are charging for the same or similar items you intend to sell on your site. This should give you an idea of the profit margins that will be involved with the items you're intending to sell. If you discover that you'll have to sell for low margins on most of the items you intend to sell, you might want to rethink the niche you have chosen.

3)   Select a platform. With your dropshipping business, you'll have plenty of platforms to choose from. I'll outline three of the most popular platforms here to give you a good idea of what is available to you.

Doba has a huge selection of products and suppliers for you to use in your dropshipping activities. They have over 2 million products to choose from. These products come from nearly 200 suppliers. In working with Doba, you will not have to partner with multiple dropshippers. Doba charges $29 a month for its basic program and a 99 cents per order fee. They have live training webinars for newbies and they'll send you email updates regarding supplier discounts, new products and seasonal products, and new suppliers as they become available to you.

Oberlo is a platform which is tightly integrated with Shopify. It allows for easy one-click import of AliExpress products. Please know that Oberlo works only with Shopify stores and it only supports AliExpress for now. They offer a free account, but with the free account, you will be limited to 500 products and 50 orders per month. When your orders exceed 50 orders a month, your monthly fee will go to $29.90.

Dropship Direct has over 100,000 items from more than 900 brands for you to choose from. It's free to use, but as you grow your business, you'll note that they have a back-end management system that is available for $37/month or free to those who are doing over $1000 a month in sales.

Other dropship platforms that might merit a look include **Wholesale2B, Megagoods, SaleHoo, Sunrise Wholesale, Wholesale Central, and National Dropshipper.**

4) **Build your ecommerce site.** After you've determined which platform you're going to use for your dropshipping activities, you'll need to develop a website or a store on which to sell the products you've chosen. Most dropshipping newbies use Shopify for their ecommerce store. Shopify has a web-based site builder that will allow you to get your dropshipping business up and running quickly. You won't need a tech background to launch a website on Shopify. And with a Shopify site, you'll have complete control over your site's navigation, content pages, and design. Also, Shopify has a built-in payment processing system that will allow you to accept payments from customers who are purchasing items on your site. And Shopify has multiple apps which will help you in developing a successful dropshipping business. Additionally, Shopify has a number of pricing plans for you to choose from. Those plans start at $29/month and Shopify will take 2.9% of sales and 30 cents per transaction on top of the monthly fee.

5) **Drive people to your site.** Once you have your ecommerce site up and running, your work isn't finished. You're going to have to continue to work to get people to visit your site. You'll do this on social media, in your blogs and vlogs, and with emails. I have outlined most of these marketing activities in the chapter on affiliate marketing, so I won't repeat them here. But I do emphasize the importance of making people aware of your site, not just once, but on a continual basis. If you have good products to sell at reasonable prices, the key to growing your business will revolve around your ability to get people to visit that site.

Chapter 5—Get Richer While You Sleep

In this chapter, I'm going to show you some additional passive income streams to help you earn even more money while you sleep. Maybe you can even get to a point where you'll be making so much money while you sleep that you'll want to sleep all the time. Just kidding. (joke)

Amazon FBA

Amazon FBA stands for Fulfillment By Amazon. Amazon FBA has become one of the most popular ways to earn income online. There are almost 2 million people selling on Amazon worldwide. About half of the sales on Amazon come from third-party selling; of the top 10,000 Amazon sellers, about two-thirds of those sellers use FBA.

Here's how it works. You send your products to Amazon. They stock them and store them for you. When a customer orders one of your products, Amazon then picks, packs, ships, and tracks that product for you. They also handle all returns and refunds. Amazon then pays you every two weeks for any of the merchandise you have sold. In return for their efforts, Amazon charges storage fees and fulfillment fees.

There are a number of major advantages to using Amazon FBA to sell your items. Most importantly, they offer you immediate access to millions of potential customers. Over 300 million people have purchased from Amazon; they have over 90 million Amazon Prime members. Bottom line, no other company can even come close to offering you access to this many customers. And because of all the packages it ships and all the warehouses it has in different parts of the country, Amazon is able to ship and deliver items less expensively than anyone else. One of the biggest reasons people use Amazon is because of the free shipping they offer to their Prime customers and also to their non-Prime customers who place orders that achieve a minimum dollar amount. Also, Amazon is well-known for its prompt shipping, its great customer service, and its generous return policy. All of these things have allowed Amazon to build its reputation as a retailer, and the volume that Amazon generates shows the confidence that consumers have in the company.

If you're going to use Amazon FBA, you should be aware of the various fees associated with it. If you're just getting started, Amazon has an individual plan for those people who sell less than 40 items per month. There is no subscription fee for this plan. (Item-selling fees obviously still apply.) If you're selling more than 40 items a month on Amazon, the next step up is their professional selling plan, which has a monthly subscription charge of $39.99. (Again, item selling fees apply.) Individual plan sellers on Amazon pay a fee of .99 per item sold and variable closing fees of .45 to $1.35 per item. Professional sellers pay variable closing fees and referral fees ranging from 6% to 25%, averaging 13%.

If you're going to participate in Amazon's FBA program, you'll pay storage fees for Amazon to store your items in its warehouse. There are short-term and long-term storage fees. Short-term fees are monthly fees that vary depending on the time of the year the items are stored. From January through September, you have to pay about .65 per cubic foot; during the holiday season, October through December, you have to pay $2.40 per cubic foot. In addition to that, you'll need to pay long-term storage fees for any of your items which Amazon stores for over a year. Amazon takes what they call an inventory cleanup every February 15 and August 15 and they'll then notify you of any items you've had in their inventory for over a year. But you can avoid long-term storage fees if you submit a removal order and get those items out of the Amazon warehouse. Thus long-term storage fees should not be a major concern. Either way, it will also behoove you to stay on top of your inventory so you can minimize monthly storage fees and eliminate the possibility of any long-term fees.

In reviewing Amazon FBA success stories, I've noted that the biggest success stories involve sellers who are selling unique products or product niches. If you want to get rich selling through Amazon FBA, you'll want to have an extremely unique product, possibly even an item or concept that you have created. For example, Amazon FBA success stories include a man who created a toy card game and another man who created a concept on flipping used books for a profit. Still another man took an old concept that had lost steam and marketed it to a new audience. He took a pop-up basketball hoop and net that had previously sold in arcades, fairs, and bars, and remarketed it so it was targeted for home use. Someone else worked with a Chinese manufacturer to develop a line of ultra-comfortable shoes, while another scouted and made available a line of health products for pet lovers. And yet another selected trendy items that he could privately label and made them available. As you can see, most of these success stories involve unique products or concepts. If you have an item like this or if you can find one, you could have tremendous success on Amazon FBA.

All You Need to Know About Peer-to-Peer Lending Opportunities

Peer-to-peer (P2P) lending is another way you can make passive income, by using your money to make more money. For those of you unfamiliar with peer-to-peer lending, let me describe it to you. With P2P lending, individuals loan their money to individuals or small businesses that are looking to borrow money. In essence, P2P is non-bank lending which cuts out the middleman—the banks. P2P lending has become attractive to yield-seeking investors who are looking for alternatives to replace lower yield traditional investments such as savings, bonds, money market funds, and certificates of deposit.

If you're saying that you don't have money to invest, I should point out quickly that you won't have to invest large amounts. Many popular P2P lending companies, including Prosper and Lending Club, require a minimum investment of only $25 in each loan. Peer-to-peer lending generally offers a rate of return that ranges from 5 to 11%. P2P lending is generally considered safe, but, as with any lending, there is some risk involved, as the loans offered are unsecured loans.

Here's how P2P lending works. A person (or business) looking to borrow money goes to a P2P lending site and fills out an application that includes the reason they want to borrow money and the amount they are looking for. P2P loans range from $1000 to $35,000. That information is then made available to prospective investors who can choose what loans they invest in. Loans are priced and categorized based on numerous factors, including the prospective borrower's credit score, current income level, the requested loan amount, and the desired term of the loan. It's important to note that almost all lending platforms do not entertain sub-prime borrowers. In fact, most of the lending platforms require a minimum credit score of 600 to 650 and they typically don't make loans to people or businesses that have had recent bankruptcies, judgments, or tax liens.

With P2P lending, the platform handles all of the administrative tasks involved in the loans, including underwriting, closing, distribution of the loan, and collection of the monthly payments. In return for that, the lending platforms take a management fee (usually 1%) for their role in administrating the loan. This management fee is subtracted from each monthly payment. With P2P lending, all the investor has to do is to select the loans they want to invest in.

As mentioned above, there is some risk in investing in P2P loans. The main risk is the possibility of default. As these are unsecured loans, you could stand to lose the money you've invested if the borrower defaults on the loan. And there is no FDIC insurance on these loans. So, worst-case scenario, the money you invest in P2P lending could decrease instead of increase. Another thing to remember is that these investments have limited liquidity. So, once you've invested, you probably won't be able to get your money out until the term of the loan has expired.

In going into the details of the possible risks of P2P lending investment, I don't do so to discourage you from participating in this form of investment. I just want you to beware of the possible pitfalls which are associated with P2P lending. Most lending platforms will rank the risk involved with each loan and some of the platforms allow you to invest in all of their different risk categories. This allows the investor to diversify his portfolio and the offset higher risks with lower risks.

I've listed some of the most popular lending platforms for investors with a brief description for each:

Prosper is one of the most popular P2P lending platforms. It allows investors to invest a minimum of $25 in a loan. Prosper has seven different risk categories that have estimated returns ranging from about 5% to 13-1/2%. It allows investors to spread their risks out over all categories so they can diversify their portfolios and balance their overall risks.

Lending Tree is another popular site. With Lending Tree, you can invest as little as $25 in any loan, but you'll still need to transfer a minimum of $1000 into your account. With this platform, if you don't want to select loans manually, they'll let you choose a platform mix or a custom mix.

Peerform has 16 different risk categories. They allow investors to invest in whole loans or fractional loans. Also, they'll allow you to spread your loans over the different risk categories, so you can diversify your portfolio and average out your risks at a level you're comfortable with.

Here are some other popular platforms you might be interested in: Upstart, StreetShares, FoundingCircle, and Kiva. StreetShares and FundingCircle target small business loans. Kiva targets loans for non-profit organizations.

40 Ways You Can Use Your Skills or Interests to Earn Passive Income

This will be fun. In rapid-fire fashion, I'm going to throw out some quick ideas on how you might use your skills or interests to earn passive income. I won't spend a lot of time or space on these ideas, as that would take an entire book itself. However, I'm hoping that at least some of these ideas will be helpful to you. I offer a wide range of ideas and I'm offering them randomly. You'll realize immediately that some of the ideas are not for you, but hopefully some of them will spark some interest for you.

Passive Income Ideas

1) **Take Online Surveys.** You can make money in your spare time by completing surveys online. There are lots of online research firms that will pay you to complete surveys. Start with **Survey Junkie** and then if you still have extra time, register with other companies.

2) **Freelance Writer.** Are you a writer? If so, you can make extra cash by writing articles, blogs, books, web copy, etc. Start with **Upwork** and **Contently.**

3) **Freelance Editor.** Are you good at editing? If so, you can make money editing blogs, thesis papers, articles, web copy, books, etc. Again, start with **Upwork** and **Contently.**

4) **Paint Houses.** Do you like painting? Are you good at it? If so, you should be able to make some extra cash painting houses, inside or out. Your client buys the paint, but you'll have to supply the other necessary materials.

5) **Sell Your College Class Notes.** If you take good notes, you can probably make some extra money by selling notes to students who are taking the same classes the following semester.

6) **Sell Your Plasma.** I did this when I was in college. Unlike blood, which can be donated only every eight weeks, you can sell your plasma up to twice a week, at $25 to $50 per session. If you have a plasma center near you, this is a great way to earn extra cash. Most cities now have plasma centers. If you are attending a large university, there is almost certainly a plasma center nearby.

7) **Sell Your Photographs.** Are you a good photographer? Do you like to take photos? Well, you can sell those photos to stock photo sites and you can sell the same photo again and again. Who buys these stock photos? People buy them to use on websites, in blogs and newsletters, on book covers, etc. It's expensive to hire a photographer, and many people prefer to instead purchase photos from a stock photo site. Start with **istockphoto, SmugMug Pro,** and **Shutterstock.**

8) **Make, Grow, Sell Things at Farmer's Markets.** Do you have a farmer's market in your community or a surrounding community? If so, these are great places to sell lots of homegrown or homemade items, including fruits and veggies, baked goods, crafts, quilts, and homemade honey, syrup, or salsa. Check out the nearby farmer's market and see if it offers you the possibility of selling any of your homegrown or homemade items.

9) **Sports Tutor.** Are you knowledgeable about sports? If so, you might consider being a sports tutor. If you are a good baseball player, you might consider offering your services to teach kids how to improve their hitting skills. Were you a quarterback in high school or college? Teach aspiring quarterbacks how to improve their throwing skills. Tennis? Soccer? Gymnastics? Many parents are willing to spend money to have their kids improve their sports skills.

10) **Math Tutor.** Along the same lines, if you're good at mathematics you can sell your services as a math tutor. I have a daughter that did that for middle school kids and she earned some nice part-time income tutoring kids in math.

11) **Second Language Tutor.** Again, along the same lines, if you are proficient at a second language, you can teach/tutor students to learn another language. And with all these tutoring ideas, you should note that you can do that tutoring in person or online, individually or in group sessions. A friend of mine has a son who is paying for his post-college trip across Europe by teaching English to Chinese students online.

12) **Voice-Over Work.** Do you have a good voice? If so, you can earn extra money doing freelance voice-over work. Start with **Upwork** or **Fiverr** to find your gigs.

13) **Get Paid to Shop.** Many people now use personal shoppers for a variety of reasons. Some people use personal shoppers to do their holiday gift shopping (I saw that in a Hallmark movie). My neighbor

Passive Income Ideas

lady is 92 years old and she pays a woman to do her weekly grocery shopping. Some corporate executives who don't have much time to spare will hire someone to run errands, such as picking up dry cleaning.

14) **Handyman Gigs.** Good handymen are hard to find. If you're good at fixing things around the house, you should consider hiring yourself out as a handyman. Start with **Angie's List, Takl,** or a classified ad in your local newspaper.

15) **Housecleaning.** You can earn extra cash by hiring yourself out as a housecleaner, either on a continual basis, such as once a week, or you can sell your services to people who are moving and may not have time to clean their places properly before leaving. Again, start with **Angie's List and Takl.**

16) **Housesitting.** Yes, some people will let you live in their homes for free if they are going to be gone for extended periods of time. No parties, please.

17) **Yard Work Services.** Some people are not interested, not able, or don't have the time to do their own yard work. You can fill the void by mowing the lawn, shoveling snow, cleaning gutters, raking leaves, trimming bushes, etc.

18) **Sewing Services.** Are you good with a sewing machine? Can you mend clothes or shorten a pair of trousers? If so, you can make extra money at home sewing. Also, please note that some people make extra cash ironing or pressing clothes from their homes.

19) **Babysitting.** A great way for a responsible high schooler or college student to earn some extra cash.

20) **Pet Sitting.** Along the same lines, many pet owners don't know what to do with their pets when they are going away and can't take their pets with them, as the rising popularity of pet hotels shows. If you're a pet lover, this is a good way to earn some extra income. Put the word out.

21) **Dog Walking.** Yes, some people don't have the time to walk their dogs. This offers you an opportunity to make some money and get some exercise at the same time.

22) **Teach Exercise Classes.** If you're an exercise buff, you can earn extra income teaching exercise classes such as spinning, yoga, Zumba, CrossFit, etc. Make money while staying in great shape.

23) **Phone-A-Friend/Welfare Check.** One of my neighbors started a company in which she does a daily welfare check on elderly persons. She has assembled a nice roster of clients and calls each person at the same time every day. Her services are mostly paid for by the daughters or sons of the elderly person who are concerned about the welfare of the elderly parent.

24) **Crafts.** Are you good or could you be good at a particular craft? If you handmake jewelry, leather goods, clothing, etc., you can sell your items on various crafts platforms. Start with **Etsy** as the place to sell your items.

25) **Small Engine and Motor Repair.** Are you good at fixing small engines? Lawnmowers, snowblowers, boat motors? If so, there's money to be made in doing so. Same goes for simple appliances such as washers, dryers, refrigerators, etc.

26) **Photography.** Are you good with a camera? If so, you might hire yourself out for special events such as weddings, anniversary celebrations, proms, family holiday card photos, family pet photos, etc.

27) **Music Lessons, Musical Instrument Lessons.** Are you a good vocalist? Good at the piano, the drums, the guitar? Earn extra cash by giving lessons to people trying to become better singers or musicians.

28) **Dance Instructor.** Are you a good enough dancer to be able to teach it? Are you good enough to offer lessons to a couple who wants to learn or refine their dancing before their wedding day?

Passive Income Ideas

29) **Mystery Shopping.** Many national retail companies have mystery shopping programs in which they will send an anonymous mystery shopper to see how their customers are being treated. You can get paid to visit restaurants and retail locations. Start with **Best Mark** or **Market Force** to see what mystery shopping opportunities are available in your area.

30) **Window Cleaning.** This is another job that people will pay other people to do. Window cleaning requires a minimal amount of tools.

31) **Computer, Electronic Device Repair.** Are you good at this? Many people are willing to pay a nice fee for someone to repair their computer or other electronic devices. A lot of times, these are very simple problems and the customer simply isn't tech-savvy.

32) **Caricature Artist, Face Painter.** My niece is very talented at drawing caricatures. She can sketch a caricature in about 10 minutes and would often take her easel and pencil to various major events around town and offer to do sketches, for a fee of course. She did that at major concerts and sporting events. Also, she went to the beach on days when a lot of people were there and offered to do caricature sketches. Along the same lines, she learned how to face paint and then used that skill to make extra money at college football games.

33) **Design T-Shirts.** Do you have a knack for coming up with designs for things like t-shirts, bumper stickers, coffee mugs, etc.? If so, check out CafePress. You can place your designs for sale on that site; and then, when customers order a t-shirt with one of your designs, you'll earn a portion of the profits. CafePress will ship the item to the customer and collect the money. You won't have to do a thing other than to load the design.

34) **Private Cooking Lessons.** Are you a great cook? If so, you can earn some extra cash by teaching other people how to cook. Maybe some people will just want to learn the basics of cooking. Others might

want to learn how to make desserts or bake pies. Others might want a crash course in Italian cooking or French cooking. You get the picture. You can make extra money teaching others what you're already good at.

35) **Organize Homes or Offices.** Are you good at organizing things? You can help people get rid of the clutter in their homes and offices.

36) **Website Design.** Are you an expert at web design? If so, your skillset offers you a great opportunity to earn extra cash. And you can do it all on the internet. Looking to get some web design gigs? Start with **Upwork** and **Fiverr**.

37) **Drive for Cash.** Do you have a reliable car? Know how to get around in the city you live in? You can make money by driving people to their destination. Many of you have heard of **Uber** or **Lyft**. If you'd rather not drive people around, there is an on-demand delivery service called **Postmate** in which you will be paid to deliver groceries, restaurant meals, liquor store orders, etc.

38) **Videographer.** Have a video cam? Good at turning pictures into videos? Then you should be able to make cash as a videographer. Start with special events like wedding receptions, birthday parties, anniversaries, family and class reunions, etc.

39) **Graphic Design Services.** Most small businesses can't afford expensive ad agencies to design their various marketing materials. But if you are proficient at graphic design, you have the opportunity to earn extra cash as a designer. You should be able to find some design gigs on **99 Designs**.

40) **Home Staging.** Can you make a home look attractive, inviting, and welcoming? It's common knowledge that staged or decorated homes sell much faster and for more money than empty homes. If you enjoy doing this, contact your local real estate agencies to see if they would be interested in this service. You'll also have no problem in

working for multiple agencies, as the homes will already be listed by a specific real estate agency by the time the house is staged.

Chapter 6--Make Killer Investments

In this chapter, I'll provide you with beginner's information on three other passive income revenue streams: stocks, CDs (certificates of deposit), and real estate. I'm detailing these passive income opportunities in the final chapter of the book, as, in most instances, these are "use money to make more money" opportunities. Although large amounts of money are not required for any of these activities, you'll need to at least have some money to start with to participate in these investment opportunities.

How to Start Investing in Stocks

If you've never invested in stocks, it's important for you to know that investing in stocks isn't as complicated as it might seem. There are now many easy to use tools available to help you invest in stocks, whether you want to take a hands-on or hands-off approach. If you're considering investing in stocks, one of the most important things to remember is that investing in stocks is a long-term game. It's not meant to be a get-rich-quick scheme. In other words, you shouldn't invest money in stocks that you might need in the short term. This includes any emergency funds you might have tucked away. The reason for this is that many stock investments will fluctuate and, if you need to get out of these investments because you need cash for other things, you'll be subject to wherever the market is at that time. And, if the market or your stocks are down, you may even lose money on your original investment. It's been proven that most stock investments will continue to increase in value over time, but the market will fluctuate and you'll want to make sure you're not in a position where you have to withdraw your funds when the market and your investments are tracking down. As a rule of thumb, you should be comfortable parting with your money for at least five years. Why five years? That's because history shows that even if the market takes a downturn, it's very unlikely that a downturn would last longer than five years.

If you've yet to invest in the stock market and you're wondering if you can invest even if you don't have much money, the answer is yes, although there are some challenges. These challenges can be overcome, but you need to be aware of them before you begin investing. The first challenge to overcome is that many stock investments require a minimum. The second challenge involves diversification. With stock investing strategies, it's common practice to diversify your investments so you will not have "all your eggs in one basket". If you have limited funds, it's going to be difficult to spread your limited funds around.

The solution to both of these challenges is to invest in stock index funds and ETFs (exchange-traded funds). For those of you not familiar with exchange-traded funds, you should know that ETFs are investment funds traded on the stock exchange, much like stocks. ETFs hold assets such as stocks, commodities, or bonds. While mutual funds might require a minimum investment of $1000 or more, stock index fund minimums tend to be lower and ETFs tend to be even lower than index funds. As a matter of fact, some brokers offer index funds with no minimum at all. (Fidelity and Charles Schwab are two of the brokers that offer index funds without minimums.) So, not only are index funds available without minimums, they also have a built-in solution to the diversification problem, as index funds consist of many different stocks within a single fund.

If you're interested in receiving a passive income stream for your stock investments without having to sell the stocks you've invested in, you might consider dividend stocks, stocks that pay dividends. Well-established companies such as Target, Pepsico, Exxon, or Disney are more likely to pay dividends than some of the newer and less-established companies. The more established companies no longer need to invest all of their profits into growing the company and they can afford to pay out profits to their investors. On the other hand, newer companies, especially tech or biotech companies, are a lot less likely to pay out dividends, as they want to use as much of their profit as possible to expand the company.

There are two main types of dividends—cash dividends and stock dividends. These dividends are often paid quarterly, although some are paid monthly or semi-annually. Dividends offer a way for companies to distribute revenue back to investors and one of the ways investors earn a return from investing in the stock. Cash dividends are paid per each share of stock that you own. For example, if you own 20 shares in a company's stock and that company pays $2 in annual dividends, you will receive $40 per year for your stock shares. Some companies pay stock dividends instead of cash dividends, so instead of getting cash from your investment, you'll receive additional company stock. You'll then be able to sell that stock if you wish to get cash or you'll be able to keep it invested in the company. Some companies offer dividend reinvestments programs, called DRIPs, in which investors are allowed to reinvest their dividends back into the company's stock, often at a discounted rate. So, if you are interested in receiving a passive income stream from your stock investments, you'll want to specifically choose dividend stocks for your portfolio.

Now that I've given you some basic information on stocks, you should be ready to start investing. Here are some simple steps to get you started:

Determine if you're going to be a hands-on or hands-off investor. If you want to be heavily involved in choosing the stocks you invest in, you're going to need a stockbroker. I'm going to recommend three different brokers that are well-suited for beginning investors:

1)   **Merrill Edge.** A good choice for beginning stock investors, as no minimum deposit is required. Charges $6.95 per trade.

2)   **TD Ameritrade.** Another good choice for beginners. Like Merrill Edge, no minimum deposit required and a $6.95 charge per trade. Currently running a promotion in which trade charges are waived for 60 days, but with a qualifying deposit. With any broker you're considering, please check their sites to see what promotions they are offering. These promotional offers are always subject to change, so what's offered one month might next be available the next month.

3)   **E-Trade** requires a minimum account balance of $500, but they also have a promotion offering a cash credit, up to $600, for a qualifying account deposit. $6.95 charge per trade.

If you don't want to be heavily involved in selecting the stocks you invest in, you should consider using a robo-advisor account instead of a stockbroker. Most major brokerages offer robo-advisors, as they are extremely cost-efficient for the casual investor. In using a robo-advisor, you can get all the benefits of stock investing without having to do all the research you would have to do if you selected the stocks that you wanted to invest in. Robo-advisor services cover complete investment management. When you go to register for a robo-advisor, you'll be asked a series of questions regarding your investment goals. From that information, the robo-advisor will build a portfolio that fits with your goals and objectives. Here are three different robo-advisors which are well-suited for beginning investors:

1) **Wealthfront.** $500 account minimum with a 0.25% management fee. Please note that the 0.25% management fee is substantially less than you would pay a human investment manager.

2) **Betterment.** No account minimum with a 0.25% management fee that can be free for up to a year with a qualifying deposit.

3) **SoFi.** $100 account minimum with 0% management fees.

One other note before we move on from stocks to CDs: One of the best stock investment options for beginners is mutual funds. Mutual funds offer an easy and low-cost way for you to get your feet wet in the stock market. An S & P 500 fund is a great place to start. For those of you that have heard the term S & P fund, but don't know what it means, an S & P fund is a fund consisting of stocks from the 500 largest US companies. If you invest in an S & P fund, you'll be purchasing a small slice of 500 of the country's most successful companies. As these companies are already proven entities, you'll be investing in a group of companies that is likely to continue to thrive.

In a similar vein, if you are using a robo-advisor, the advisor will be able to create a portfolio of stocks from successful companies with which you'll be able to own a sliver of each of these customers and diversify your portfolio. These are low-risk stock investments, as the companies you'll be invested in will be proven entities.

All About CD Laddering

Before we get into CD laddering, I'll define what a CD is. A CD is a certificate of deposit. It is a time deposit that is commonly sold by banks, credit unions, or thrift institutions. CDs offer a very low-risk alternative to people who are looking to get higher interest rates than the meager interest rates they get on their savings accounts. The trade-off is that with a savings account you can generally take out your money at any time without a withdrawal penalty. With a CD, you will not be able to access your money for the length of the deposit, whether it is a one-year deposit or a five-year deposit.

CD laddering is a very simple process. CD laddering involves purchasing multiple CDs at the same time, with each CD maturing at different times. e.g., 1-year, 3-year, 5-year. Instead of placing all of your CD money in the same time interval, you will choose different intervals. CD laddering offers total flexibility. You can purchase different amounts for different intervals; you can even choose different banks for your different CDs, depending on the interest rates offered by those different banks. For example, if you have $10,000 to invest in CDs, you could invest $3000 in a 1-year CD, $3000 in a 2-year CD, $2000 in a 3-year CD, and $2000 in a 5-year CD. Maybe you use one bank for the 1- and 2-year CDs and another bank for the 3- and 5-year CDs because they are offering a higher interest rate than the first bank is offering on those intervals.

CDs already guarantee a rate of return. By laddering, you can get even higher interest rates and you'll always be close to having money that is available for any unexpected emergencies.

Let me give you another example to show how you can earn additional interest by laddering your CDS. Again, let's say you have $10,000 to invest in CDs. If you invest all $10,000 in 1-year CDs and continue to roll those CDs over as they mature, on an annual percentage yield of 2.8%, you will have increased your $10,000 to $11,502.68 in a 10-year period. On the other hand, if you take that same $10,000, and invest $2000 each in 1-,2-,3-,4-, and 5-year CDs, you'll get the higher interest rates as the length of the term increases. If you are getting the 2.8% interest on a 1-year, 2.95% on a 2-year, 3% on a 3-year, 3.05% on a 4-year, and 3.15% on a 5-year, you original $10,000 will have increased to $11,668.36 after 10 years.

Four Simple Ways to Make Real Estate Investment Income

Investing in real estate offers lucrative opportunities for you to earn additional passive income. One of the exciting things about investing in real estate properties is that, unlike stocks and bonds, you can pay for just a portion of your real estate investment before you can begin making money from it. Normally, you'll pay 20 to 25% as a down payment for the real estate you purchase. In some instances, you might even pay as low as 5%. Regardless of what your percentage is, from the time you sign your mortgage papers, you'll be able to start earning money from that investment.

Let's look at four simple ways you can make money from your real estate investments:

1) **Become a landlord.** If you buy a house or a small commercial property, you'll be able to make money by renting out that property. The upside of this is obvious. You'll be able to use your renter's payments to pay your mortgage. In many instances, you will be charging your renters a monthly rent that is more than your monthly

mortgage payments. So, not only can you make money on your monthly payments from a renter, you can also use them to make your mortgage payments and increase your equity in the property as the property is probably appreciating.

In all fairness, there are some possible negatives involved in being a landlord. Unless you pay a company to manage your property, you'll be stuck with handling any problems at that property. If the hot water heater goes out, you'll be responsible for replacing it as soon as possible. If the washing machine, stops working, you have to either get it fixed or replace it…in most instances, at your expense. If you rent to bad tenants, it's possible that they can damage or destroy your property. If they don't pay their monthly rent, you're still going to have to make your mortgage payment and you might even have to pay to evict those tenants. If you can't rent your property and it's vacant, you're still going to have to make the mortgage payment.

That said, if you ever get to a point where your mortgage is paid off, the rent you collect will become almost all profit. At the same time, as you own the property for a period of time, that property is probably going to appreciate and you'll have a much more valuable asset than you started with.

2) **Real estate investment groups** are a great option for people who want to own real estate but don't want the hassles of being a landlord or managing a property. In a typical real estate group, a company buys or builds a set of apartment buildings or a condominium complex. They then allow people to purchase the units within those building or complexes. A person who buys a unit then becomes part of the real estate investment group. A single investor can own one or multiple units in the buildings or complexes, but the company operating the investment group will continue to manage all units, handle all maintenance, advertise vacancies, and secure tenants, in return for a certain percentage of the monthly rent. If you are in a real estate group and your particular unit has a vacancy, you'll still receive a monthly payment, as any vacancies will be covered by the entire investment group. As long as there are not a lot of vacancies in the building or complex, you should still be able to derive monthly income from the unit(s) you own.

3)   Real estate trading (flipping). This is the wild side of real estate investing. Real estate trading is very risky, but it can also be extremely lucrative. Flipping is not for the "weak of heart". If you're going to be successful at flipping, you are most likely going to have to be good at evaluating real estate and then marketing that real estate. There are two types of flippers. The pure flipper is interested in buying properties that require very little or no alteration. They will simply want to resell the property for more than they paid for it. The other type of flipper buys reasonably priced properties with the idea of renovating them or improving them to a point where they can then be resold at a profit. This is often a longer process than pure flipping, but profits can be substantial. If you're going to do this type of flipping, you're going to have to be willing to secure contractors who can renovate the property and you're going to have to be willing to oversee this work. Some people get into flipping without an idea of who to hire or what it is going to cost to make the improvements they want to make to give the property more value. If you've been hooked on the TV shows that revolve around house flipping or if you've been reading some of the tremendous success stories regarding flipping, you should know there are also many stories out there concerning newbies who expected to make their fortunes by flipping homes, but got in over their heads and had a disastrous flipping experience

4) **Real estate investment trusts (REITs)** are basically a more formalized version of real estate investment groups. A REIT is created when a corporation (or trust) uses investor money to buy and operate income properties. Unlike the aforementioned real estate investment groups, REITS include non-residential properties or real estate ventures, such as shopping centers, malls, and office complexes. REITs are bought and sold on the major exchanges, just like stock. With REITs, a corporation must pay out 90% of its excess profits to investors as dividends in order to maintain its REIT status. In doing this, REITs do not have to pay corporate income taxes, whereas a regular company would be taxed on its profits and then have to decide whether or not to issue dividends to investors from its after-tax profits. REITs are considered to be a solid investment for investors who want regular income.

Conclusion

Is there a better time than now to start earning more money? With all the passive income streams I've provided you in this book, you can no longer say that you don't have any ideas as to how you can earn some extra money. No one would ever pretend that all of these ideas will suit you, however there are definitely some ideas that you can pursue. Now the question is, are you going to spend your time complaining that you don't have any extra income streams or are you going to do something about it? I've given you the tools to be successful. What you do with those tools is up to you. When you were a kid and got a brand-new toy for your birthday, did you wait to use that new toy? I'll guess that you started playing with that new toy immediately. The same goes for the ideas in this book. Surely, you found at least a few good ideas among all the options I presented. Excuse the analogy, but now that you've read this book, the bus has just dropped you off at the road to success. Are you going to get on that road or are you going to get back on the bus?

Whether you use your money to make more money or whether you simply use your skills to make money, it's time to start now. I doubt that you would have read this book if you were not interested in making more money. Yes, most of the ideas presented will require some time or effort on your part. However, if you are willing to put in the initial effort, many of the ideas presented will allow you to earn extra money, some of it while you sleep. Checking your bank account balance can become something you look forward to instead of something you'd rather not do at all.

Whether you embark on micro-investing, blogging, peer-to-peer lending, or just walking dogs, there's no better time than now for you to start earning more money.

NO MORE PROCRASTINATION

Simple Habits to Boost Your Productivity & Get Things Done. Discover How to Eliminate Procrastinating Habits & Overcome Laziness for Good

Table of Contents

Introduction 105

Chapter One: Quit Bad Habits Now.. 109
   The Biggest Misconceptions about Laziness *109*
   5 Reasons Why You Are Lazy And How To Fix Them......................... *111*
   6 Ways to Overcome the Lazy Brain *115*
   7 Terrible Habits that Keep you from Success *118*

Chapter Two: Firing Up A Motivated Mind... 122
   Which Type of Procrastinator are you? *122*
   10 Must-Know Hacks for Mind-Blowing Motivation *129*
   The Fixed Mindset vs the Growth Mindset... *133*
   5 Tips for Developing a Mindset That Brings You Success.................. *135*

Chapter Three: Getting The Job Done.. 138
   11 Essential Techniques to Power Up Your Productivity *138*
   10 Secrets Behind Productivity According to the World's Billionaires *143*
   5 Time Management Strategies to get More Done in Less Time *147*

Chapter Four: Sharpening Focus 151
   14 Exercises To Develop Razor-Sharp Focus *152*
   The Crucial Link Between your Brain and your Belly *159*
   5 Ways to Develop Unwavering Self-Discipline.................................. *161*

Chapter Five: Goal Setting For Success 165
   Concepts Associated with Goal Setting.. *166*
   Forms of Goals *167*

10 Goal-Setting Techniques to Achieve your Goals Faster.................. *167*

7 Things you Need to Know About Setting the Right Goals *171*

The Best Ways to Reward Yourself for Completed Goals *174*

Chapter Six: New You, New Routines **178**

8 Ways to Create Great Habits that Lead to Success........................... *179*

9 Morning Routine to Make Every Day a Good Day *185*

6 Evening Routines to Ensure Tomorrow is just as Good as Today. ... *189*

Chapter Seven: No More Obstacles **192**

7 Ways to Conquer Your Fear of Failure.. *192*

7 Strategies for Defeating the Monster of Perfectionism *195*

7 Ways in Which Positivity can Manifest Success................................ *198*

5 Empowering Mantras to Destroy Self-Sabotage and Start Getting Stuff Done. *202*

Conclusion **205**

Introduction

It doesn't matter what phase of your life you are currently in, or what profession you may find yourself.

The truth is that all of us are all trying to overcome procrastination in one way or the other.

We yearn to not only get results, but to get them fast. Results are good, but the faster they arrive, the better for us. And this is where procrastination comes in.

Most of us already have everything planned out. Our heads a bubbling with a lot of ideas and visions, and we want to get started as soon as possible, but procrastination holds us back from achievement. It is so subtle that you never know that you are being held back.

Most people who procrastinate actually end up completing their tasks before the deadline, but they mostly face the pressure of completing a job under pressure. A procrastinator is never satisfied with the completed job even when it was completed before the deadline. There will always be this fear that something was not done right. Procrastination forces you to live in anxiety and perpetual fear.

There is hope. The first step is to understand that there is a problem. A procrastinator that doesn't know that he/she procrastinates is on the way to the largest pitfall in the world. Knowing you have a problem is the beginning of the solution. Procrastination is tricky, but it can be understood. You only have to make up your mind that you want to understand. And that is what I will be helping you do in this book: understand procrastination.

You can only break its stronghold only after understanding what makes it strong. There are little bits that can help you overcome procrastination. Do you know that the content of your stomach at any given point can have an effect on your productivity at that time? Surprising, right? But that is the case.

As you follow my guides in this book, I want to assure you that you are in safe hands. I am Ethan Grant, and I love to think as myself as a productivity agent. I am a leading speaker on the topic of productivity. I understand both the concept of productivity and procrastination, and I know how to switch them in a person.

There is something I refer to as the procrastinator psychology. It is so strong in procrastinators that they hardly ever know it exists. I will be revealing that to you during our journey through the pages of this book. I only ask that you stay with me and be as attentive and proactive to change as ever. I have designed this book in the simplest form possible so that it can benefit anyone who reads it. The steps listed are all practical ones, so you will have problems following them.

Toni Morrison noted in one of her books, "If you surrender to the air, you can ride it." There are a lot of possibilities in your life. The quantities of things you can achieve are quite overwhelming, but procrastination will never let you.

If you have ever sat down to imagine all the great things you COULD have done but didn't do, even though you are 100% sure you have all it takes, then, you should know you have a procrastination problem. But once this problem is overcome, a lot of possibilities begin to open up to you, things you had never imagined you could ever do.

The benefits of conquering procrastination are numerous. Just sit and try to imagine all of the fulfillment and purpose that could come to your life if you decide to take a step today and become productive in whatever field you may find yourself.

My productivity tips have touched lives in various places. I have people call and tell me some of the ways in which my teachings have affected their lives very positively. Over the years, I have toiled endlessly to produce some of the nuggets I will be sharing with you in this book. You should count yourself lucky because you will be receiving most of my life's work in the following chapters. These are nuggets that have changed lives and created a fresh path for people who had once been frustrated in their frustration.

Productivity is a blissful thing, but it has to be understood and respected before it can be applied. Of course, nothing good comes easy, so you will have to give the procedures in this book some time before you begin to reap the benefits. But I can assure you that if these principles are applied, there is nothing that will be able to stop your light from shining.

You might be asking, 'Why this book, out of all the other books that deal with the topic of procrastination?' The major aim of writing this book is to pour all of myself into these pages. You won't just be reading a book; you will be picking my brain and going away with wonderful knowledge.

I am a seasoned teacher, and I try to be as technical as possible with any of my written works. This is to make sure that my reader easily understands the information I am trying to pass across. If the communication gap is faulty, then, the whole writing venture is utterly pointless. It is this communication gap that I have tried to bridge in the best way possible. The method listed here are procedures that a determined person can use successfully without any stress.

Remember, Heaven only helps those who help themselves. Sitting under an apple tree does not mean you will go home with a basket full. You need to take action and plug down some for your satisfaction. Success is right there at the corner, but she will never come into your house until you ask her in. And, dear, she can be very selective, only listening to those who understand her principles.

Finally, remember that our world only belongs to action-takers. No real change can happen except you decide to take action. Action is the key ingredient in every success story. You have to begin to beat procrastination now before it snatches away your glorious destiny.

A productive lifestyle should be your major aim as you strive to become a better version of yourself. Begin to practice all the tips and guidelines provided in this book and don't falter. Results take time to come back, and it is only the steady that stand to reap the benefits of their labor. I hope you soon have a positive story to tell. Good luck as we dive in.

Chapter One: Quit Bad Habits Now

The Biggest Misconceptions about Laziness

Let's start by noting that laziness is not a sickness or a personality disorder; it is mostly something you have accepted for yourself. Laziness is something that slowly creeps towards you, entangles you, and gradually takes over your personality. It is very stealthy, and it works hand-in-hand with procrastination.

Think of laziness as a desire of the layperson. It is something you want to do, something you are very comfortable with. Although a lot of people might argue and talk about how much they hate laziness, deep down inside of them, there is a part of them that is comfortable with just lying around and getting nothing done. It is almost like an inner conflict with yourself. One part of you is begging you just to achieve nothing, while the other part knows and understands the repercussions of those actions.

Take note that laziness and rest aren't the same. You rest after completing a huge project, but when this rest continues for an extended time, then you know that there is a problem. Laziness can so eat up into a personality that it becomes part of their personality, a habit that they can do nothing about. And this is where it gets weird and dangerous. At this point, the individual might begin to see laziness as a disorder or a sickness, which in most cases, is wrong.

The habit of laziness can form from a variety of circumstances. It is even more active in adults who have somehow lost motivation to be adventurous and seek out new things in the world. Study the children around you. You hardly see a lazy one. They are always up and doing, looking for the next big adventure and discovery. And that is why life stays bright and true to them because they understand the rudiments of new things.

On the contrary, laziness in an adult can result because the older person believes he has seen enough of life and is now particularly unmotivated. This is laziness of the mind. Here, the individual in question is endowed with enough strength and energy to carry out the task, but because there is no zeal, the task remains undone. And laziness is blamed.

From another perspective, laziness can be said to be a variety of states which can be emotional or physical that can affect a person's zeal to get things done. For different people, there are different reasons why they are lazy. Sometimes, laziness can spring up in a hardworking individual all because of lack of interest. Imagine an extreme introvert and extreme extrovert, both planning for parties. One will definitely put in more effort into the preparation more than the other. Now it is not that the introvert is lazy, but introverts are generally people who do not like to invest in social activities.

But this shouldn't be an excuse to accommodate laziness. A person is never born naturally lazy, except if there is a sickness that naturally weakens the individual. Apart from that, laziness is learned or walked into and becomes a habit. The funny thing about laziness as a habit is that it continues to grow on you until it completely destroys all of your plans. Laziness is one aspect of your life that can affect another part of your life and ruin it with laziness. If you get away with laziness today, your mind will try to trick you into believing you will get away with it again until the devastating finally happens.

5 Reasons Why You Are Lazy And How To Fix Them

Many times, people have a bleak sense of the fact that laziness has finally crept into their life. It is no longer a question of 'Am I lazy?', but now 'Why am I lazy?' While this is a very important question, the answer to that question is not readily available except through a deeper search. There are various reasons why people end up lazy, and these reasons vary from individual to individual. Laziness can be caused by a wide range of external factors, including psychological.

A lot of revelation has been given on how to overcome laziness. Like other traits, laziness can be pulled off one's skin and replaced. Although this method works, most times the candidates applying them may drop back into laziness. But there is something quite deeper to the situation. You have to sit and understand the true cause of your own brand of laziness before a solution can be prescribed.

There are some generally identifiable causes of laziness in different individuals, no matter their personality differences. Some of these include:

1.   **Being overwhelmed by the task at hand.**

Some people get overwhelmed by the size of the work required to complete a project. One method to get rid of this is to break down major tasks into smaller tasks, but even this itself can cause a person to ignore the task. Most times, people lack the knowledge required to go about breaking down a task. So, they just forget the task and leave it hanging. This form of laziness mostly has to do with mental capability. It is laziness that is formed because an individual cannot do the mental exercise required to understand the task at hand.

This task will require an insane amount of research, materials collection, and all other requirements. But the solution here is to learn the skills involved in breaking down a task into smaller tasks. It is not a skill that one is born with. It is developed over time, with constant practice. If you have identified this kind of laziness in your life, it is time you put effort into learning how to deal with large projects and handle it in parts, one at a time.

2. Unidentified Purpose

Unless you have established the reason why the completion of a particular task will be important to you, your mind will never put the body to the task of completing the job. When there is no clear-cut purpose, there will hardly be any motivation to complete the task. Laziness easily seems to be a safe haven for people without a clear-cut purpose to pursue.

Once a person becomes plagued with such a form of laziness, there will be no zeal to act. All that they will be looking for is a form of escape, something that will relieve them of the thought of purposelessness. If you discover that you fall into this category of laziness, the solution will be to find something that motivates you. Find something that will make you want to act. Before you start any task, sit, and list out all of the benefits you can get when the task is finally complete. This will provide you with some motivation to get the job to the next level.

3. A need to produce a perfect job

No More Procrastination

For a perfectionist, the rule is to get it done to 100% excellence or leave it undone. While this can sometimes be a very admirable trait necessary to produce the best results from a task, it can sometimes dampen a perfectionist's zeal to work. A perfectionist will spend hours and days gathering and perfecting the material requires to start up a task. The non-perfectionist, on the other hand, has already begun with what he has and has made progress. In time, he will be through with the job, putting the finishing touches to perfect the job as well as he could.

Perfectionists always get frustrated easier while working on a task because attaining perfection is never an easy task. There will always be factors on the ground that ensure that the work never attains perfection. The fear of making mistakes is another factor that holds perfectionists from starting up a task. This happens most especially when there is a portion of the job that they are not fully capable of carrying out. So, to prevent mistakes, they don't even start at all. While this might not outrightly translate into laziness, when it continues to build up, the person can begin to lose the zeal to work.

You can curb the effects of this perfectionist lifestyle by understanding that perfection is not attained in one go. It takes time to get something to be as good as you may want it to be. And that is the beauty of working on something, to put in more and more until you create something of quality. Quality takes time and effort. The joy is in the process of completing the job, and you will be fully rewarded when it is achieved. Understand that there is a time to set aside your perfectionist mindset and try to get things done, even if you are not too confident in your ability to complete the given task. Don't be scared that people will look at you differently when you fail. They, too, have failed before, so you shouldn't mind their glances. Just do what needs to be done.

4. Accepting laziness

There is a kind of laziness that is inhabited, laziness that you can speak yourself into. Some people have never put their minds into achieving something tangible, such that they don't even have an idea of what it is to be productive. It is more like a state of complacency and inactivity. These have a mentality that before a task can be carried out, it has to be fun and enjoyable, so whenever they are faced with a tedious task, they blank out and look for ways to escape. Things that do not fall into the enjoyable category are left for later, and then later, and finally later until they are never done.

Having these thoughts once in a while is completely normal. That is just the way your body works. But if it keeps on recurring over and over, then you know that they are a problem with your work ethic. Your body only wants to enjoy itself, which is wrong. There should be times when your body will be disciplined and made to get the job done. These thoughts can, in some ways, block your ability to produce something worthwhile, something that can be appreciated.

Strip your mind of these kinds of thoughts and get to work. See yourself as someone who has to achieve. Action taken now is always the best, and it will lead to the most satisfying rewards.

5. Health conditions

Like has been noted earlier, there is a kind of laziness that is caused by physical ailments or sickness. If you find out that you easily feel tired and there is never any motivation for you to work, then you should consider having yourself medically tested. These sicknesses hardly ever reveal themselves until it is quite late, but your body responds to them early enough, and it is left to you to detect these responses. One of such ways the body responds is to feel tired to help you conserve energy. Yet that shouldn't be the case. All of these could be as a result of a thyroid disorder. These thyroid problems could lead to diabetes, heart diseases, and other sicknesses that could weaken the body.

6 Ways to Overcome the Lazy Brain

When laziness becomes attached to a person, it can also affect their brain and make it lazy too. Your brain and your mind, most times, work hand-in-hand. And once one of them begins to accommodate the notions of laziness, the other is instantly affected. This is known as mental laziness.

Mental laziness can present itself in a variety of ways. For one thing, mental laziness can appear in the form of a disorganized and scattered mindset. Your mental faculty will always be in disarray, producing a lot of varying thoughts that mostly have no meaning. Most of these thoughts that occur as a result of the mental disarray are:

- Negative thinking.

The mind is mostly conditioned to think about the wrong things about life, always to ruminate and consider the things that have gone wrong. How do you expect to produce results when your mind is clogged with such thoughts? It will be very hard to achieve that. These negative thoughts can build up and affect you mentally, psychologically, and physically. Once your lazy brain tells your body that it is sick and it cannot perform, your body obeys and falls into laziness.

- Missing the most important things in the picture

A mind flooded with thoughts is a mind that will always be in a panic. Nothing ever stays stable. This can kind of thinking will always draw you into yourself, causing you to miss the things right in front of you.

Some of the ways in which you can control this lazy brain and bring it to book include:

1. Guard your mind

Be a gatekeeper for all of the thoughts that pass through your mind. Observe the thoughts as they come and go and try to figure out the pattern in which they occur. You will be able to identify the negatives and positives. Probe yourself and find out why negative thoughts have become incessant. There may be small reasons lurking around, which you may need to fix. It could be anxiety, fear of failure, or mental stress.

2. Pay attention to each thought.

As the thoughts come to your mind and try to produce laziness, pay attention to each and every one of them and find their root. If you are anxious about something, then find out why anxiety occurs in the first place. If you are stressed out and can't perform optimally, then try to find out how to combat this stress and restore your body to its normal functioning state. Eliminate these thoughts one by one and reduce the power of the lazy.

3.   Don't look for an escape.

Most people are always on the lookout for things that will help them escape the present and live in a parallel universe of entertainment. While it is OK to seek some form of escape from the hustle and bustle of life, it should be checked if it becomes too much. If you find out that you are that kind of individual that relies heavily on entertainment to escape and avoid the 'disturbances' in your life, you will notice that your mind will soon begin to experience deterioration.

There are other forms of escapism that people employ to release themselves from the grip of their lives. These recreational drugs only offer you short-term pleasure and heightened consciousness. Once it wears off, you are faced with the same issue that you had been trying to escape from. Your best option if to face whatever it is head-on and conquer it once and for all.

4.   Stay Mindful

Being mindful entails paying full attention to the things around you, both those that have to do with your mental state and those that have to do with the physical world around you. Don't let anything, no matter how small and infinitesimal it may be, pass you by. Enjoy life yet probe yourself and identify reasons why you enjoy certain things. While doing this, make sure to allow your mind some room for exploration. Allow your mind to wander a little, but don't allow it to travel too far lest you lose it.

5.   Get Organized

Disorganization easily results in clutter, and clutter in any form is not only a distraction but a huge wet blanket. Having your personal space clogged with clutter can result in loss of motivation. A clean space always invites you to work, to get something done. A disorganized space, on the other hand, pushes you away and tells you nothing can be done.

Try to observe it for yourself. How do you feel walking into the kitchen and meeting a pile of plates waiting for you in the sink? It is natural that you would want to attend to that before putting else on fire. The mind is always more comfortable and able to organize itself to produce whenever it is presented with a clean space.

6. **Seek help when necessary**

There is always help for you in trying to cure your mind of laziness. All you have to is to search for it. Sometimes you might not be able to get over a distraction or temptation to stay lazy single-handedly, but with the help of others, you will find it easy to do. There will naturally be this fear to meet people for help. This might be because of an unpleasant experience in your past, but it is a necessary skill to be learned, especially when struggling with something as addictive as laziness. A little practice may be needed to acclimatize you with the basics of finding help.

7 Terrible Habits that Keep you from Success

To live a life of productivity is to become successful in whatever you may find yourself doing. And habits themselves are some of the factors that build up to produce success. It is our habits that define us that make us who we are, either as success stories or as a failure. This is why it is necessary that one builds the perfect habits to enable success. Sadly, most people have spent their lifetime building habits that foster failure and push them further away from success. Here, I will be highlighting some of those habits that could hinder your success.

No More Procrastination

1. **Inability to say 'no.'**

Sometimes you should be the bad guy and do some rejections. Not everything you are invited to participate in should be participated in. If you find it hard to say no and not feel guilty about it after, you will realize that you have stressed both your body and your soul. Also, if you keep on saying yes to everything, you will have an overwhelming schedule, which can turn out to be disastrous too.

Research has linked depression to an inability to say no because you will soon find out that you can no longer control yourself. Not saying no can derail you from your main goal and have you chasing something else simply because someone else had cajoled you into doing that.

2. **Fear of risks**

Play it smart, but don't play it safe. That is something I love to tell my students. It is natural to nurture some fear about your future, but you should never allow it to affect your work and the decisions you make. To fear risks is to ensure that you never get anything tangible. The best things will always elude you. And no matter how much you fear risks, that thing you fear will still befall you one day, so it is best to take the risk anyway. Take risks and fail and know that at least you learned something new. That is the beauty of life, to explore and discover new things.

3. **Held back by your past**

They say, "let bygones be bygones," and I couldn't agree more. Forget the thing in your past, the things of failure, and the things of success. Success, too, has a way of holding you back from achieving more. If you have achieved it before, then, you should forward and try to conquer more. Don't allow yesterday's success to prevent you from doubling your efforts and doing more. The same goes for failure too. The best thing you can do for yourself if to bury things of the past and look forward to the future.

4.   **Building your life on mere talk**

This habit is deadly. It is for people who will spend most of their time talking about a vision instead of actually getting to work to make it happen. Talk is good, but the action is better. Do you know what is best? Getting to action immediately. Don't allow the sweet stories in your mouth clog up your mind until you begin to ignore the main work that has to be done. Talk is cheap, and action is expensive. Don't live a cheap life. It is dangerous.

5.   **Playing blame games**

Blame is a heavy burden, and it is a beautiful thing to get it off your shoulders. You instantly experience freedom, and you can go back to relaxing. It stays sweet until it becomes too late when you finally discover what the damage of throwing blames has cost you. If you are to be blamed, there is no need to reject the blame for the sake of temporary freedom. Accept your blame and move forward with it. Instead of making excuses and trying to free yourself, try finding out why that venture failed in the first place. Throwing blame around is a recipe for more failure.

6.   **Lack of self-discipline**

Self-discipline is simply obeying yourself as your own boss. Self-discipline is stooping low so that you are humble enough to listen to your own self. You should be able to talk yourself towards success and out of failure. In fact, you can never succeed if you have not learned how to scold yourself when necessary. Apart from that, you should fear the deadlines you place. There should be punishments for not completing a task at the right time. These are some of the things that self-discipline entails. In the end, it is all about being your own toughest master and teacher.

7. **A competitive mindset**

Subscribing to healthy competition is suitable for your development, but when competition begins to lead to envy and low self-esteem, it becomes dangerous. Your major completion should be yourself. Improve yourself irrespective of the success of others or what they are embarking on at the moment. Allow other people's success to become a motivation to drive to work, not to drive you insane. Stay in your lane, but ensure that you make that lane the best it can be.

Chapter Two: Firing Up A Motivated Mind

You might be surprised that, while things might get tough, only now, you lose the drive to continue because it is just about you. Of course, the only "being" you see around is your inner self. And even your inner will to push forward has been stricken with a deadly disease I call frustration.

Do not fret! You eventually get to that stage. In fact, it is a big sign that you are progressing. It shows that you have scaled through the starter's level. Although the progress might appear slow and it might not mean much compared to the goal you have set to achieve, you are now in a position where you need to get motivated.

Be careful not to express this feeling of frustration into your daily life. The consequential effect is that nothing will seem to work for you. Why? Because you have preconditioned it as a reality to live with.

Two things might set in, discouragement and procrastination. Discouragement because you are not sure if it's going to work. And procrastination because your progress is slow. Neither of these is a deal to settle for, and other harmful things might follow.

This chapter will explore all you need to know on how to keep going.

Which Type of Procrastinator are you?

It will be interesting to note the importance of productivity at our workplace and in our daily lives. But one thing that destroys our creative ability to do more is procrastination. Procrastination is simply the act of pushing the accomplishment of things to the future; things you consider of less value in your present moment.

We all have been in this pool before. Admitting this fact doesn't present it as a good habit to do. Although prioritizing might redefine the content of the tasks pushed to the future, it only shows that we have been able to identify the root of age-old difficulties. Some might tend to shift responsibility to another time because they feel that they are incapable of doing such a task. Others might just be to fulfill another act of laziness.

1. The Evader

There are times when we are at our best to accomplish a task. But sometimes, we just decide not to continue because we worry that we can't do it. Self-doubt then kills creativity in us. You are scared that you might flop, and the only thing that comes to your mind is to push it forward. No one will argue the fact that it is good to recognize our limitations and weakness. It is also necessary that you don't allow it to hold you back.

Build a sense of importance

Understand the value attached to the task you avoid. See those values as commitments that need life support. Of course, you are the one who secures its existence by accomplishing it. And since life support is not a decision to avoid, your tasks shouldn't also. You may tend to compare each of those jobs you push further as your heartbeat. As much as our heartbeat is essential in the future, it is considered as of greater importance for the present also.

Breaking out of the evader

- Outline a positive outcome

Create enough reasons not to avoid the task. The joy of achievement alone should be a constant motivation to spark you up. While you have been a continuous benefactor of the satisfaction and pleasure derived from not doing it immediately, you can also get that fulfillment when you think of it positively.

- Gear up your will

Everything inside you must receive the right knowledge to do things quickly. And the good thing about willpower is that you are the best influencer.

- Start in pieces

Work can be overwhelming sometimes; but with strategy, it will become interesting. Break down the process of completing the task into parts. Don't think of achieving it in a stretch. Allot each piece with a time limit, say for 5 minutes (you are in control here). You might need to declutter your bedroom. Give three minutes to arrange your sneakers and two minutes to sort out a tie. Going with this flow makes the job quite more manageable and exciting.

2. **The Stickler**

Excellence is a virtue that should be seen in everyone; but it shouldn't affect the completeness of a job. Some people are stuck in the circle of bringing out the best in everything they do. They can't do less until they are satisfied that the work is world-class.

No one is negating the just essentials of doing things in the best way; it proves the importance of productivity. But understand that in many cases, the attention required for such tasks needs to be well monitored; and so, we tend to push it forward because we are overwhelmed. There is this fear of low standard that denies them to start off immediately.

Breaking out of the stickler
- Do the analysis

Mathematics wouldn't be necessary here, but you can think of doing the arithmetic of the last job you did. Ask yourself different questions ranging from when you started to how did you complete it. Was there any consequential effect attached to it? Were you able to attain a 100% success rate? Was there any reward of internal satisfaction to this? What outlook did it give your job? It is more likely that you have been too hard on yourself to perfect your next task, and that's why you want to fix the slightest details.

- Have a clear intent

Understand the nature of the work to be done. The technicalities, modules of operation, design outlay, and presentation. Be sure to have a clear definition of what you need to achieve. When your purpose is clear, you will not be distracted.

- Define your satisfaction

A functional analysis would make this step easier for you. Once you have been able to itemize what your happiness is, looking for it in every job you do would not be a problem again. Your satisfaction might come when you achieve, say, the right mix of color in your interior designs.

3. The Cluttered Brain

Yes, clutter! It might be true that we are really busy with many things to do. Ranging from work to social group activities, religious commitment, health and safety checks, family upkeep, and so many more engaging routines. Multiple office tasks alone at your workplace might be a threat to prioritize your daily job. It then becomes a problem to choose the right task to do at the moment. And when this gets too much for us, we tend to do some tasks and push others to the future. Sometimes, our mental state is as busy as our workload that we get confused from within first, then the reality of the physical adds insult to injury. It is apparent that you are occupied with many things to do, and the slightest time to rest is also used to think. You would agree with me that those thoughts aren't as productive as they should.

Breaking out of the cluttered brain

- Set priorities

Identify the most relevant job at hand and do them immediately. Don't ever get overwhelmed when minor tasks seem to be the large chunk of the situation. Create an express list of your routine tasks. Do the ones you feel is both necessary and urgent right away, and steadily complete others.

- Determine a deadline

As much as the job is essential, it is vital to set a time limit for each of your task. Taking too much time on a particular problem leaves others piling. Note that your time limit must be achievable. Since most of your works are routinely done, devise a strategy to simplify the process.

- Work with facts

Seek the counsel of the experts on specific tasks. Taking a step like this gives you an edge to succeed at a faster rate. Work with proven facts and figures from professionals and ease your workload burden.

- Delegate responsibilities

You don't have to necessarily do all the work. Seek the help of a colleague or, better still, allow your office assistant to do a part of the job. Be careful, though, in delegating power. Ensure that you take the critical decisions and monitor the progress of any delegated duties.

4. Carefree

These people do not see any reason to do a particular task at its proposed time. They feel that there is enough time to do the job. Fun is being derived from this act, and nothing seems to make more sense than taking hands-off work.

Remember when you needed to write a college report for a field trip, and the experience from this exercise encouraged you to plan for the next one? What happened is that you spent a lot of time fantasizing about the next trip but not into writing the report. So, the time meant for the critical task of getting the description ready was used for something else which might not be as important presently.

A fraction of this group believes that they are most effective when the deadline is close. So, they feel pressured to put in their best at the very last hour.

Breaking out of the carefree

- Do statistics for arithmetic

You might not be familiar with this principle. It's simple. Since you really don't see a reason to do the most crucial task at the moment, try applying the same principle to what you would have done at that moment. Try procrastinating your fun-filled activities. Experimenting on this will give you another sense of urgency to undertake tasks.

- Count the effects

You might need to be truthful to yourself here: What you really want is fun. But how much has this fun cost you? Think of a greater sense of accomplishment you would have had if you don't push the task to the future. There is no harm in attempting something good, so give it a try.

- Examine your triggers

You might not be aware that the source of your procrastination is not really you, but what you do at some point. Your environment might be a trigger. Do a brief examination of the things you do and see if you can do them in another way. Apply the same principle for your tasks too. It might interest you to discover what pushes you to procrastinate.

5. The fantasizer

If you belong to this group, it means you have spent a lot of time having plans but didn't take any constructive step to accomplish it. It looks quite easy to talk about reading five chapters of a book per day. In fact, you might have initiated this whole idea to your colleagues, but the stage of presenting it was the last effort made to achieve it. Understand that a proposed action without a constructive strategy remains a fantasy.

Breaking out of the fantasizer

- Understand goal setting

Starting with a plan is not a wrong move, just that the approach to achieve it must be accurately spelled out. Goal setting takes a commitment of not giving up even in the face of distractions. You will need to take every suggestion given in Chapter Five of this book seriously.

- Start small

There is no need to rush to get to the height you have always imagined. Take your time to do your task. Remember what you want to achieve will not come automatically.

- Get real

Stop wasting time on what is not achievable. If what you have always planned to do is unrealistic, its time to cut them short and get real.

10 Must-Know Hacks for Mind-Blowing Motivation

Excellence is a thing to think of when aiming at achieving goals. Lots of factors would need attention to actualize this, and one of them is motivation. Motivation is that force that keeps you going in the face of challenges and distractions. To meet your targets, you would need to keep moving to enhance your productivity level and boost your performance.

1. Begin Little

One big killer of achievement is when you don't see yourself doing more, especially the way you have fantasized it. It wouldn't come as you thought. Understand that what should matter most to you whenever you are starting something new is progress.

It might look tiresome because you feel you are not moving at the same pace as others'. That might be another mistake also. This is you doing your own thing, so you don't have any obligation to work at anyone's speed. Checking other people's progress should inspire you to do more, not to enslave you into regret.

The reality of a long-term goal is that it requires a long period to be achieved. So take it slow and steady until you finally meet your targets. You don't need to fret.

2. Identify a Strong Purpose

You shouldn't undertake anything when you have not outlined the intent. It is necessary because this will serve as a reminder any time you want to give up. Your purpose should be firm and essential to you. This assurance is what upholds your willpower.

Your intent might stem from your childhood experience, goal setting, career choice, family background, and so on. Whatever it is, it must be convincing to you. Be careful not to be enticed by the environmental factors. Don't take a course of action because that is the trend in your immediate environment. Be sure that you have thought about it very well and you are ready to go through it.

3. Design a Structure for your Goals

You need to differentiate yourself from everyone else. Remember that your intentions have a deadline, so nothing should distract you from fulfilling it. Create a guide that will help you focus. It can be an express outline of your targets or a picture containing what you want to achieve. Doing this brings clarity of purpose. You then know every input/resource needed to achieve success.

With a structure, you will be able to track your progress at every point in time. If it is necessary to report to anyone, your composition would have mapped it out. You wouldn't get tired of achieving an outstanding result because your progress is evident. Having a well-defined structure makes you advance in the essential details. It is a sure model for motivation.

4. Add Fun to your Task

No one is encouraged to do more when everything seems tedious, especially when it is a routine task. Position your job as part of your life that deserves happiness. And an excellent way to stay happy while doing your work is when you add fun to it. You don't have to be rigid here, and your job might not necessarily be a treat.

Also, don't forget that discipline should not be a lamb to sacrifice for pleasure. Play your favorite playlist while you type and enjoy the rhythm. You may also decide to chat with your colleague during your break. Speak lavishly about what makes the job interesting.

5. Look Out for your Tribe

Tribe here means people of the same kind. It might be a colleague that has decided to be on the same course of action with you. You might have decided to write a review for five international magazines on a particular theme. Check someone around you who have made the same decision too.

You will get more inspired because you are sure that you are not alone on this journey of success. Seeing the other person(s) creates a mindset of competition. Make it more fun when you meet with them by challenging your abilities. Your aim here is not to feel awkward even if you don't meet the target given to you. The teamwork spirit should get you going.

6. Avoid Negative Thoughts

Naturally, diverse ideas will flow through your mind, whether you are doing well or not. But you can sieve whatever comes to your mind. Be in control of what dominates your thoughts, especially negative ones. A better way to maintain good ideas is to have positive affirmations whenever a bad one flashes in your mind. You might be thinking of not achieving the task because you feel you are incapable. Tell yourself that "I am not deficient of abilities, and I will have productive and outstanding results."

7. Learn more

Task yourself to learn about a particular task. The good thing about knowledge is that it set you further beyond expectation. Many people have actually gone through what you are thinking of doing. Read about them. Learn the different challenges they faced and how they overcome them. Reading their stories will position you to have extensive experience as you won't need to fall victim to the circumstances. Read newspapers, magazines, and blogs; watch videos, and get yourself inspired by your discoveries.

8. See a Professional

Their job is to guide you through extraordinary sessions. Your aim here is not to limit yourself to what you hear. An encounter with the experts makes the job more personal. You will be able to relate your fears, frustrations, and challenges with an open mind. At the end of the day, you must have been held accountable for the procedural counsel. You could also sharpen your leadership skills with a professional. And if the success of what you want is a priority, don't think about the cost attached to seeking the help of a professional.

9. Step Back Frequently

Working smart is the key to a successful work outcome. You don't have to get stuck over a task for too long just because you want to find a solution. Restore your mental capabilities by taking breaks. Your health is most valuable when you need to get going. You would agree that you are less productive whenever you spend more time than necessary. You might be trying to design a book cover, but it seems the dots are not connecting. Leave the job for a while. Take a walk down the street or probably surf the internet. During that break period, your brain and other parts of your body would have been refreshed, leaving you better than before.

10. Live Healthily

No one can take care of you better than you. Look out for nutrient-giving foods. You might consider eating vegetables and fruits, depending on your diet. Taking water frequently is quite healthy. The focus here is that your physical body must be able to sustain every activity you intend to do. Living in sickness is enough discouragement to perform any task.

The Fixed Mindset vs the Growth Mindset

The subject of mindset is important because what we make of it determines our productivity level and success rate. Mindset is the collection of ideas (stemming from personal to environmental, cultural, and spiritual experience), assumptions, beliefs, and thoughts held up to become a constituent part of inclination, interpretations, disposition, and mental habit. It is then crucial to master the art of mindset both for personal or professional use. The effect of mindset is shown at the behavioral level and creates a rigid perspective about life in general.

The Fixed Mindset

As the name implies, a fixed mindset holds that their daily-life attributes are static traits, and therefore cannot be modified. People with this mindset focus more on what they can do as fuelled by their intelligence, ability, and talents. Any effort that leads to success is not an option to them. They somewhat vouch on their talent alone instead of adopting strategies to improve and build it. You might have seen people who have limited themselves on the extent of performance; those already have a perspective of "I can't change."

An example of someone with a fixed mindset is one who believes that he is an athlete because he can sprint to some extent. The mindset would be known during training sessions. If he insists that he can't break the track record but can only maintain his current streak of performance, then he is susceptible to be one.

The fixed mindset does not see opportunities to get better at what they do, and they put no effort to improve. You may have come across people who are dogmatic about using some modern facilities just because they were raised by their grandparents, and must have been misinformed. Whenever there is any change, then it is not for them.

Also, consider when a student is taught how to solve a particular problem in Mathematics. If the facilitator adds variables to the question, then explaining it conventionally becomes a problem (something a fixed mindset will give up on because he felt the other way around is the best way to solve it), so, he gives up.

He could have accepted his weakness in not knowing the problem and then looked for a way around it. The change in the question posed a threat to him already, and he felt helpless, and that was enough reason to give up. If he were asked why he gave up, it would be easy to point fingers, go defensive, and retaliate.

The Growth Mindset

A growth mindset accommodates changes to improve skills and qualities through perseverance, dedication, and effort. People with this mindset believe in all-around development by building strengths and abilities, not just where they feel they have the ability.

These people have an understanding that learning can be developed with persistence. Although when failure comes, it is with an understanding that it can get better, and not an avenue to shy away. They have an insight into the realities of possibilities.

People with a growth mindset are most likely to work at their full potential because challenges do not make them stop, but instead put in more effort. For example, one out of five foreign students in a German class has difficulties in the language. A growth mindset will not get discouraged because he didn't meet the standard of others, but will understand that he just needs to give more effort. Patience will be another thing to take note of here.

5 Tips for Developing a Mindset That Brings You Success

1. Create a Platform to Learn Something Different Every Day

The dependency of fixed traits will not breed a world-class result. Take time to speak with a professional in the line of your strength and ability. There is always a better version of your power. The expert should be able to guide you effectively and push you to do the right thing at every needed moment. Take the pain of learning and doing something different from your immediate talent every day. You may also consider reading about what you learn online or join a friend who wants to learn the same with you

2. Expand your Learning Experience

It is super cool to hear of one's assessment from people. But when it becomes a habit, then you need to be wary. You don't have to focus on getting approval from people around you. It does not matter what they think or say about what you do. Channel that energy into learning. Learning should be your priority and follow the procedures patiently. Bear in mind also that education is a process, and it may not come easy as you would expect. The learning experience will keep you going to achieve great results.

3. Reference Weakness

You must know where the problem is coming from. It might be triggers or just your community of friends. Enough of the excuses for failure and dejection! Embrace your weakness by acknowledging it. This will be the first step in liberating yourself to the world of growth.

4. Be Open to Different Eventualities

Challenges would definitely come, but you have to be prepared for it. Prepare your mind to see the goodness in every difficulty. Learn to weigh your options. Always consider using "what if." You might have decided to read for three hours a day, and it seems unachievable. Ask questions and challenge your routine. What if I have not been following my guide? What if I need to be more specific? What if I need to take breaks? What if I check my diet? What if I read about people who have done the same thing?

5. Reflect Daily

You should be in charge of disbursing the truth to yourself. Have time to meditate on your course of action. You might find it interesting to do this at night when you are done with the work for the day. Analyze those thoughts that have limited you to underperform and how you can overcome them.

Chapter Three: Getting The Job Done

Productivity entails a lot of things, and one of the most important of them is about getting things done. As easy as it may look, a lot of people still have problems getting things done at the right time and in a complete manner.

This is where the understanding of productivity comes into play. To be productive is to understand tips and techniques and know-how to apply them accordingly. Productivity works like a system, but it doesn't just go into action.

In this chapter, I will be guiding you through some of these factors that can help you become more productive. The techniques and tips I will be revealing to you will yield viable results for you if only you decide to use them unflinchingly.

11 Essential Techniques to Power Up Your Productivity

To understand ways to build productivity, it is necessary that one understands the meaning of productivity. They are many misconceptions about the term, and if they are not handled, the whole essence of this chapter will never be accomplished.

First of all, bear it in mind that productivity isn't only about ticking boxes off your to-do list. It is more than that. Productivity, in this sense, basically entails getting the right things done in the right time frame in the most effective way possible. Having the perfect system to help you boost productivity is very necessary for both your work life and your family life. You definitely stay ahead of things when you understand the mechanisms that fuel productivity.

No More Procrastination

The building blocks of productivity is in setting up realistic goals and achieving them one step at a time. At the end of the task, you should be able to ask yourself, "Did I do something meaningful with the space of time allocated to me?" If the answer is yes, then congratulations are in order. You have been productive.

One major reason why people fail at being productive is that they have too much going on for them. Being able to select the right task for you and going after them headlong is a very special and important skill that you should learn. There a whole lot more techniques that are quite important when trying to become more productive, and I am going to walk you through some of them. Follow these techniques closely, and watch productivity take a great leap in your life.

1.   The Eisenhower Matrix

You will most definitely need a pen and paper for these techniques because you will have to draw out a quadrant. The first two quadrants at the top of the four squares will be tagged "very important." The next two underneath will be tagged "less important." But the first two quadrants from the left side will be tagged "urgent" while the next two quadrants at the right will be tagged "less urgent."

After that is complete, you can now begin to sort all your tasks into the boxes. There are those that will fall under "very important" but "less urgent." Others will be "very urgent" but "less important." It is all about understanding how to place each task. Every task that falls into "very important" and "very urgent" should be the ones that you will face quickly. Those definitely carry a lot of weight. On the other hand, those that fall into "less urgent" and "less important" are the ones that can be left for later. Assigning your tasks in all of these boxes will help you with your decision making.

2.   The 80/20 rule

The idea of the 80/20 rule comes from a business model. What it means is that 80% of all your profits come from lesser than 20% of your customers and business partners. With that, it is necessary that you know how to treat this 20 % so that they stay and keep providing you with 80% of your profit.

Bring that into your daily life and see how it translates. Notice how just a few things you do actually have a lot of impact on your life. Less than 20% of your everyday activities are enough to have a real influence on your life over a long period of time. It would make sense to place a strong focus on that 20 % so that more meaningful impact can be generated.

3.   The Five Majors

This concept was developed by the CEO of Stack Overflow, and its concepts encourage that one person should never have more than five activities on their to-do list at any point in time. Keep your lists short and try to achieve everything on the list with a short period so that you can add more activities to the list and go ahead. You should be working on at least two activities on your list, the next two should be in a queue, and the last one should be a secret task that only you know about, something you must have challenged yourself to do.

4.   Exercise your Body and Mind

Exercise frees your body and gets it ready to perform. Exercise in this form does not only have to do with the body alone but also the mind. While the body profits from your physical exercise, the mind profits from mental exercise. Mental exercise helps you to open up your mind and allow your imaginations to run wild, which is quite beneficial to your productivity.

5.   A Break will Help you

Some of the most productive people understand the power of breaks. Not only will they help your body relax and feel out new ways to relax and get things done, but they will also allow your mind to re-strategize plans. Have you noticed how the best ideas come to you when you have totally forgotten about the job? Yes, that is your brain working on its own, undisturbed by the stress of your coaxing and anxious mind. Instead of working for long stretches, set a timer and get things done in little bits. They will cumulate into one big success story.

6. **Shun Multitasking**

There are people who have optimized their bodies and minds for multitasking. It is quite easy for them. That is rarely ability, too. No one is saying you can learn it now, but don't gamble with it just yet. Take time to study yourself and find out how good you are with multitasking. Chances are, you are not very good; so it will be best for you not to venture there. Nothing kills productivity faster than a person trying to multitask. And in the real sense of things, multitasking is a form of distraction in itself. Your mind remains divided throughout the process. Just focus on one job at a time and see how far you can go with that.

7. **Love the Things you Do**

This is not easy to do, especially for people who have found themselves in jobs that they are not happy with. If you are not happy, then it means you do not love what you do, which leads to frustration. If you are not happy, it is better you leave and find something that gives you fulfillment. The truth is that you can hardly be productive doing something you do not love. If you love it, your mind will no longer view it as work, and it will be easier for you to perform the said tasks.

8. **Strangle your Distractions**

Getting rid of glaring distractions is key to increasing productivity. Every entertainment in your life is there to reduce your productivity level. Once you understand that and deal with them squarely, it will be easier to overcome them as they arrive. Tell your mind to focus on the essentials and not look sideways to the non-essentials. The funny thing is that your mind obeys you, and it, too, would like to see a specific task completed.

Find a quiet place where you can work, a place where you are sure you will not be distracted. This is the first step in dealing with distractions. If you have created a list, then tell yourself that there will be no fun for you until you have accomplished about three things on that list. Breaking our tasks into smaller bits always helps.

9. Complete the Most Important Tasks First Thing in the Morning

The best time to complete your most intimidating tasks is early in the morning when your mind is most vibrant and ready to perform. Don't put off your task until it becomes late, and then you find yourself rushing the task to complete the task. Begin before your mind starts to slack and watch yourself progress even before the day goes halfway. Completing the most taxing activities early in the morning will give your mind and body a kind of positive push to keep trying harder.

10. Create a Schedule

Don't just rush into things without a plan. A schedule will help you to streamline your activities and keep you more focused while helping to eliminate distractions. But don't forget to create time for rest and pleasure in your schedule. If not, it will never be a workable one. Take off whole hours to get yourself together and replenish your mind.

11. Reward yourself

If you have achieved anything that marks you off as productive, then you should reward yourself. Your reward can come in any form, but make sure it is something you will enjoy, something you will thank yourself for. Having rewards set in place will give you something to look forward to asking you try to complete the task as fast as possible.

10 Secrets Behind Productivity According to the World's Billionaires

There is no better place to get advice than from the best of the best, some of the most productive people in the world who are billionaires. It is not easy to control your environment, but you can learn how to do so, and this is something that billionaires are quite good at. You should sit down and try to learn from them.

The world has more than 1500 billionaires, and most of them are quite effective at time management and productivity. Don't get it twisted. These people live the same kind of lives as you. They receive thousands of emails every day that require sorting. They have thousands of employees in their payrolls, and they also have a lot of decisions to make every day. Have you ever wondered how they manage to stay on top and achieve so much in such little time? How they choose the things that are important and those that can be left for a later time? These are men and women who have built their wealth systems in such a way that they receive in excess of $5000 every day. And productivity is something they don't joke with.

Here are some of the most outlined points that they listed as some of their most important:

1.   You Don't Have to be Everywhere

The late Steve Jobs stated that to increase his productivity; he spent a lot of time streamlining the number of meetings and places he had to be per day. Some other billionaires stated that there is no need to attend a meeting or being in a place if you are sure that you won't make a lot of money from it, or talk about something really important. It is more important that you delegate someone to go on your behalf instead of presenting yourself at the venue. Most high-profile billionaires have described most meetings as a waste of time with people talking about irrelevant things.

2.   Simplify your Calendar

Your calendar here refers to your schedule. Most billionaires advise that people learn to keep their calendar simple and decongested. Instead of having hundreds of things to be done in one week, try picking out a select few to be accomplished within that week and leave the rest for the next week. It is no good trying to stuff your schedule with lots of things and not achieving any of them in the long run.

3.   Identify the Place Where you Perform Best

We are all different, and we all have different psychologies. Because of this, the areas where we most liable to perform best differ from person to person. Find your place and stick to it. What time of the day do you perform best? How should a surrounding be before you can get in the zone to work? For some people, a loud and noisy environment is the ideal place to work. For others, it will be a silent and very secluded environment where they will come in contact with very few people.

Once you find out what works best for you, build on it and enhance that environment. Some billionaires have thinking rooms built into their homes where they sit and think for hours on end; others travel to very secluded places where they can commune better with themselves. And all of these produce very wonderful results for different individuals, especially when they are practiced in the right way.

4. **Keep your Focus on the Most Important Goals**

There are goals, and there are GOALS. The key here is not allowing other less important goals to hold you back from achieving the main important goals. People who achieve a lot know how to set the most important goals and face them like their lives depend on it. This is not to say that you ignore your other dreams. Instead, keep your eyes on the big ones, those ones that will have the most positive impact in your life within the shortest time.

5. **How Well are you Doing?**

Billionaires are people that love to track their process on any project. Nothing is ever done just because it is done. They live their life intentionally and love to follow all of those intentions and see success. It is advised that you create metrics with which you can use to determine how good you are performing. Your metrics can be using a small book to write down everything you achieve or making use of software or apps that help to track process. With a fully tracked process, you will be able to look and improve your performances.

6. **Take Advantage of all the People Around you**

The people around you are some of your most important resources. It is quite neglected, but billionaires have always advised people to be more conscious of the people around them. If you are the kind of person who loves to work on your own and shut out other people, then you should learn to make some adjustments in your life. People are always around that can make your life more successful, and you should maximize them. Billionaires basically report that they recruit people to help them achieve their dreams and ideas. Getting to use people is to create more time for yourself. The job gets faster in a shorter time.

The major problem is in finding competent people; but once you are able to scale that, you will have the most productive time of your life.

7. Technology is There for you

Renowned billionaires around the world are known for their love of technology. Look what Facebook did for Zuckerberg. Look at Steve Jobs, Bill Gates, and other selected ones. Sometimes technology is your best option. Technology gets it done easier and quicker.

Automation can work in any business as long as you are able to discover a way to introduce it into your business to help you work better. All you have to do is make sure you already have an efficiently working system before you incorporate technology into your work. If not, you might end up confusing yourself and achieving nothing.

8. Create habits that help your Productivity

Billionaires are people of practice; they know how to build positive habits that help them to become more productive. Some of them are known to be early morning people; others are known to be nocturnal animals. Billionaires know how to develop the perfect habits to help them out to become more productive.

9. Set Time for the Most Important Work

Remember that activity is not equal to productivity. Don't allow yourself to get drowned in the hustle and bustle of life. There should be a set time for you to carry out the most tasking of your activities. Productive billionaires know that special time needs to be set aside to get the most important jobs done. During this time, there will be no calls, no emails, and no internet. It will be only you and the job right there in front of you.

10. Recognize your Opportunities

Productive billionaires unsurprisingly have the best eyes suited for figuring the best opportunities that should be maximized. You will be tempted to take on every viable opportunity in front of you, but not all opportunities are for you. Take time to review all the opportunities in front of you and find the ones that best suit your skills and personality.

5 Time Management Strategies to get More Done in Less Time

There is something about time management you need to know: Time cannot be managed. Instead, you can only manage the events that occur within a period of time, giving the illusion that time has been managed. Every one of us has been provided with the same quantity of time, which is 24 hours per day and 7 days per week and so on. So, the question now is, how can you fit all of your activities into this period of time so that you come out with the utmost satisfaction and remain productive?

With this understanding, it is also necessary that you note that time is also a commodity. It can be sold and it can be bought. It can also be budgeted, and it can be used with wisdom and common sense. Another thing is that time management is an art that can be mastered.

Time management strategies are affected by different factors when they are applied by different individuals. Personality, will to achieve, and the level of discipline are some of the factors that can affect a person's ability to manage time. These strategies have been proven over time to help people with managing their time. Practice them and watch your life change.

1. **Be Organized**

Disorganization and poor time management go hand-in-hand. Where one is present, the other manifests itself. Get rid of any form of clutter that may have besieged your life so that time will be spent more wisely.

There are simple ways in which you can achieve organization and a decluttered life. There are thousands of resources on the internet that can help you out, but the simple way out is to learn when to let go of things. Know what to put away and what to leave. Note that the clutter that is being referred to does not only have to do with the physical everyday clutter. There is also the mental clutter and digital clutter. All of these have a way of slowing you down and reduce your ability to manage time.

To get rid of mental clutter, make sure that your mind stays clear both emotionally and psychologically. An unstable mind is a distraction, which in turn deprives you of focus. Digital clutter, on the other hand, will mix up your files that will make you spend hours looking for a document. Deal with all of these individually and return your life to stability.

2. **Identify and Deal with Time Wasters**

Your productivity and time management is affected by a lot of external factors controlled by the people and circumstances in your life at any given moment. These factors are some of the major causes of time wastage, as they have a way of affecting you without your knowledge. All that happens is that with time, you discover that you missed something somewhere. But you have the power to either increase or decrease their effect such that they are no longer capable of wasting your precious time. Some of these factors you should look out for include:

- Uninvited visitors or guests
- Unimportant emails and letters to be replied
- The internet (social media)

- Relationships
- Little pleasures

3. Is your Time Worth Anything?

Take a few minutes and try to take stock of your time. How much is it worth to you? If it is worth something, then how can it translate into productivity? Once you do this, you will find for yourself a sense of understanding that your time should be spent wisely because of its worth. When the value of a thing is unidentified, it is easy for it to be abused and misused. Create value for your time and don't allow that value to ever be reduced. If you are going to get distracted for 15 minutes, you should be able to determine how much you must have lost during those gone 15 minutes. With that in place, you will easily be able to organize your mind and get yourself to act.

4. Care for Yourself

Taking care of yourself is one major way in which you can avoid time wastage. Take time to relax your body, your mind, and your soul. Keeping your body and mind at its best helps you accomplish tasks even faster than usual. Find out what time of your day your body performs best and maximize those periods to the best of your ability.

Mismanagement of time can manifest as a result of bodily fatigue and sickness. Depression can also cause you to put off important activities, and this is why your mental health should also be checked from time to time. As I have noted before, take time to rejuvenate your mind and reward yourself whenever you are sure you have accomplished something noteworthy.

There should be a healthy balance in your life between your work and family. There can never be any form of real productivity without this balance in place. Instead, you will spend a lot of time thinking you are productive at work while your personal life experiences failure.

5. A Necessary Sense of Urgency

To have a sense of urgency is to understand that there is no room for time wastage. It is to understand that speed is necessary when an opportunity presents itself. Develop the ability to take action and to take them very quickly. It is one thing to take the corresponding action, and it is another to take that action before it becomes too late. One thing that differentiates achievers from their opposites is their ability to take appropriate action sat the right time.

Chapter Four: Sharpening Focus

Awareness is a thing to remember when learning to get focused, whether on personal targets or on assigned duties. It is one of the tools leaders consider in achieving a massive turnout of success. The beginning of this consciousness positions leaders to direct the attention of people following them. To sustain this growth, the leader must focus on their care.

We must first know that getting focused is beyond filtering alternatives while paying attention to one. One could concentrate in diverse ways and for different purposes to pursue an available course. Being a leader here does not necessarily mean you lead in a position of authority, and you are not pushed to the thought of being one. Our priority is to ensure that you lead a proper life for yourself.

Remember that there is a larger world to give attention to; those things that connect you to the world. People following you (comprising of people you work with or for, the ones you mentor, and the ones you are accountable for) deserves attention too, and lastly, yourself.

Problems you complain of often might come from distraction, or maybe multitasking. With things ranging from meetings to work schedule, back-to-back reviews and presentations, and finally again to supervision, note how each day has become a mountain of workload. And you could barely have time to sort out your thoughts. This schedule would be reasonable if you are 100% sure of your success rate and might not need a rethink. But in the long run, you might break down both mentally and physically.

14 Exercises To Develop Razor-Sharp Focus

We would begin with those little daily tasks you often consider as of little importance. Expect to see a change as you hold the exercises with the utmost value. This mind will be the breakthrough to sustain the success of the activities.

1.   Learn your Work Structure
Increase your focus rate by understanding the details of the job. Ask questions on what is unclear. Meet your supervisor or your direct superior and make clarifications. You might want to ask for a record of such a task that has been done before. Your inquisitiveness would clear the doubt that would have misled you. And will only make you look out for the excellent completion of the job. Your focus would now be sharpened as you can now comprehend every fragment of your work schedules.

2.   Arrange your Desk
This exercise will deal with every distraction that might spring from clutter. Imagine your table is full of unfinished reports, seminar papers, minutes, and other relevant official documents. What happens is any time you see them gives you anxiety and worry. Fear tends to creep in.

Instead of allowing such unnecessary pressure from your mind, arrange or rearrange your desk as the case may be. Keep documents in their order of priority and gain some peace for your mind, if for nothing else. This action will allow you to be conscious of what is most significant at the moment, and you will be mindful of it.

3.   Stretch your Body
Mental capability is not isolated from our physical components. Your hands, leg, even neck plays a lot of role in improving your productivity

level. Note that I am not negating other parts of your body; neither do I underestimate their functions. Our attention here is the role each of your locomotive parts plays in revitalizing your body.

Practice twisting your fingers one after the other in a clockwise rotation. You need to be careful and gentle with this exercise so as not to injure yourself. Continue the rotation for five minutes and pay attention to the steady movement you are making. Fix your mind on all you notice, starting from the sound of the first two rotations to the unequal flow of the tip bone. You might see your veins and how your wrist tends to move with the spinning finger. Take time to do this with all your fingers with your mind focusing on the movement.

You might extend this practice to your hand, too. Stretch and keep your hand still for about 12 seconds and fix your gaze at the outstretched arm. You might want to try other parts of your body too. Just ensure that you pay attention to all you do.

4. A Three-Minute Study of an Insect

Insects are almost everywhere. Good places to enjoy this exercise will be in your garden and at a park. Take a walk to a park and sit under a tree. Look closely at the bark of the tree. You would surely see an insect. It might be on the grass or at the branches of a flower/plant. Any one you notice first is good to go with.

Get close to the tree or plant but not too close; make sure you look around closely so as not to disturb other insects. Study the movement of the insect(s). Put close attention to where they started their journey. You might be fortunate enough to see them carry particles (if walking with their friends and neighbors) from one place to another.

Your focus will improve if you could pick one insect out of many and use your sight to monitor it for 3 minutes. This period of mindfulness might look long to you because of their movement, resemblance, body structure, and color.

5. **Colored Bottle Study**

All you need for this exercise are different-colored bottles. You can have a mix of plastic and ceramic jars. Place them on a table and create a little distance from it. Stare at them as long you can. Start with three different colors which might be a mix of your favorite. You might tend to focus more on one color than on others; your aim is to be mindful of a specific color. The more you are aware of your choice bottle, the more your focus is strengthened.

Whenever your mind wanders away from your task, try to bring it back as quickly as possible. You may also want to write down those thoughts that flash through your mind during the process of this exercise.

6. **Jazz Music Break Down**

The genre of this music might not be your pick but listening to it will help boost your focus level. Notice that there is a soft combination of musical instruments for this kind of music. Your attention should be on the timing of each of the instruments used.

Your first assignment is to get into the rhythm. How does music make you feel? Your present environment is not your concern for now, and that's why it will be best for you to do this exercise behind closed doors. The next thing to do is to channel your emotions to your thought. To do this, bring your feelings to align with your ideas through the music. There is an emotion that follows the piano, while the drum set is different also. Just flow with the music and don't wander away.

7. Smell Exercise

This exercise will work well for those who have a strong sense of smell. But it doesn't leave out every other person. Every time there is a strong smell, try and be a detective. Exert effort to trace where the smell is coming from. It might be the smell of a coffee, perfume, flower, or even food. Let your brain interpret the scent and enjoy the feeling they bring to you. You might go further to know the intensity as in the case of food. You might want to determine whenever the food is boiling or burning.

8. Movie Report

Your kind of movie might be romance or action. Your focus on film should be on how well you can tell another person about the most exciting part. If you can do this successfully, then move a step higher by becoming the movie to talk about to a friend. Doing this will require more serious attention than the movie. You are both the actor and director here. Detailed and specific information will be required on all you do and how you do them. This exercise will allow you to comprehend your actions and will most likely expose the intent behind them.

9. Feel your Pulse

No tool will be required to carry out this exercise. For you to be successful on this one, you first need to monitor how you breathe. Put attention on how you inhale and exhale. At what rate? And under what conditions do you breathe either fast or slow? You might notice that when you are a bit anxious, your breathing changes compared to when you are confident.

Be in a comfortable position, either on the floor or chair. Make sure your body is relaxed. Take a slow, but deep breath and launch into the experience. Focus on the subtle sound of your pulse and breathe. You might also want to experience how slowly your chest expands.

The attention given at first might not be as perfect as a golden plantain. Don't be hard on yourself. Do it repeatedly and enjoy the tranquillity that accompanies the natural thought pattern of this exercise.

10. See with your Eyes Closed

Since the eye is the organ than gives sight, it is the most accessible doorway to most distractions. We don't need to pluck out those eyes to stop seeing them. But we can also rely on it to strengthen our focus.

Go to a public place but with few people around, close your eyes, and focus on your feelings. If you are successful in combining your emotions well, step further in this exercise by going to where there is a crowd. Notice the sounds around you — the footsteps, chant, and chat. Can you still concentrate on your feelings? If yes, then try as much as possible to understand what is going on around you. Once you get to this level, your mindfulness has increased to a definite high.

11. Conscious Listening

This exercise is similar to the movie report, only the group of friends involved is different. Speak to your friends about having a heart-to-heart discussion. It will be interesting if you have a mix of males and females.

Group yourselves into groups of two from opposite sexes and form a listening clique. Ensure there is a coordinator that monitors this exercise. Discuss any subject you all agree to converse with friends only. When your partner is done, switch roles and be the one to listen. Timing will be necessary for this exercise, say five minutes. When the clique is done with their first ten minutes, the coordinator then announces for both of you to share each other's story as you heard it. Ensure that you use the exact word, phrase, and possibly the gesture as you were told. Make your partner's story appear personal to you.

At the end of everyone's session, the coordinator then allows everyone to comment on their experience. At the end of this game, everyone would have been able to achieve some level of strengthened attention.

12. Conscious Eating

Conscious eating here does not mean impulse eating or feeding, influenced by emotions. It entails the awareness needed when eating your daily meals. And since food is essential for our daily nutritional needs, we could both enjoy the feelings attached to it through mindfulness. The satisfaction will come when you have an understanding of why you eat. The thought of the reason should be far from hunger. It's about building a relationship with food.

Let's start with the process of cooking and the smell attached to it. Maybe you have not been conscious enough to absorb the feelings attached to "pre-cooking and pre-eating." Your aim when eating shouldn't be to swallow. What about the coloring, the garnishing, and cutlery arrangement?

Enjoy your next meal by taking it in bits. Bite, steadily chew the food, and allow yourself to experience the feeling of each spoon. While eating, you may ask yourself if the emotion attached to it is right. Don't eat because everyone seems to be eating at that moment. You have likely been doing this before, but you might not enjoy this exercise if that is what motivates you to eat. Remember that our aim for this exercise is to be able to concentrate on every detail of what you eat.

13.   Conscious sitting and standing

We often do this without taking into account how frequently we do this. It will best describe acute mindfulness if you account for your daily activities. Sitting and standing is one that could boost laser focus ability. One is likely to rise and rest many times in a day without taking cognizance of it. Your job requirement might force you to do so.

But you could also build mindfulness in doing the same. Be in charge of the decision to either stand or sit. It might not sound easy at first, but it's worth the try, and you may even remember after you have walked a few meters. Once you register this consciousness as a new vocabulary in your mind, you will see yourself getting familiar with it.

14.   Word Count Exercise

Try this exercise with your favorite book, magazine or newspaper. Start with five paragraphs and read them. After you must have absorbed the content, begin the word count. Count each word from the first paragraph to the last and repeat the process in descending order. It will be essential for you to note each word you count. Keep to memory the usage, function, and intent. The more you do the counting, the more you are aware of the words.

You could also commit to mind the number of words in each paragraph. When you are sure of your achievement for five sections, you can proceed to 10, 20, or even a whole chapter.

The Crucial Link Between your Brain and your Belly

One crucial factor to consider when thinking of a healthy lifestyle is the food you take. The traditional benefits of food spans from medicinal to nutritional; it is the most considered build-up to all-around soundness of the body. As it is said, "You are what you eat."

Individual meals are prescribed to patients based on their illness, imperfections, and symptoms. And this has proven to be effective over time. Asides genetic factors, feeding has the capability to change the growth level of individuals. An example will be a comparison between well-fed children to malnourished ones.

There is a connection between our productivity level and the food we eat. You would agree that not eating adequately has a way of telling on the brain. Remember when you were famished; it was as if nothing is working in you. The only thought that filled your mind is the consumption of food. This feeling is not strange because the presence or absence of food has been proven to regulate your activeness, alertness, energy, and willingness. When you're hungry, your ability to focus was reduced, and your mood was not at its best.

Your brain suffers when you are hungry because it can't perform to its highest potential. You won't be able to focus on a task; and even when you do, it is most likely not to be excellent because your blood sugar level is not regulated.

1. **Almonds**

This fruit contains fiber and protein, which are known to increase feelings of fullness. Eating this nut allows you to consume fewer calories per day. It also has an antioxidant called phytic acid which protects against oxidative stress. Ensure you consume the brown layer of the skin

2.   Salmon

The presence of high omega-3 fatty acids content is what makes salmon able to boost memory and mental performance. You might not get disappointed quickly. A fish oil supplement can also achieve optimum results for depression.

3.   Green Tea

This natural tea contains L-Theanine. This property is a component that increases calmness and tranquillity. It works perfectly with another part called caffeine by making it release steadily. Caffeine boosts focus and alertness. You could stay active all day when you enjoy it in its powdery form.

4.   Bananas

Banana contains glucose which releases energy to the body. Eating a banana a day will complement the daily need for glucose. It is also great as a between-meals food as it will fill you up. You may try it with a peanut for a composed snack and experience the refreshing moment all day. The presence of pectin in banana regulates blood sugar level and reduces appetite by reducing the vastness of the stomach

5.   Eggs

An egg contains an abundance of Omega-3 fat and a B-vitamin called choline, among other nutrients. It works to enhance the mental reactive sensors and also raises the High-density lipoprotein which is connected to reduce the possibilities of many diseases

The nutrient in egg appears more as one of its calories is higher than most foods. These nutrients can help to keep the hunger away for an extended period.

6.   Brown Rice

The magnesium present in brown rice relieves stress and boosts productivity. Unlike white rice, the energy present is released slowly to increasingly build-up power throughout the day. The health benefit is contained in its whole grain form. Another fantastic component is the low glycemic index. The glycemic index shows how fast a food raises a person's blood sugar. Brown rice is rated as an average GI food making it easy to consume.

7.   **Dark Chocolate**

Once the concentration of cocoa is 70 percent or higher in chocolate, then the nutritional value is a thing to celebrate. The flavonoids found in chocolate as well as in other fruits and vegetables has an anti-allergic, anti-inflammatory, and anti-tumor properties. Flavonols also reduce the risk of heart disease, cancer, and stoke. It seeks to lower blood pressure and helps in blood flow, leaving your body active all day. Once your heart is perfect, your brain wouldn't have any issues functioning.

8.   **Blueberries**

Blueberries are noted for its antioxidant properties that fight disease, as well as able to stop belly bloat. The hidden benefit of this fruit is that it enhances cognitive ability. Your brain is set for the day with this fruit.

5 Ways to Develop Unwavering Self-Discipline

Learning does not stop at the moment of doing; it continues until the behavior is personalized. You wouldn't approve of a child's knowledge until it becomes part of the child's way of life. For example, after a child has learned cleanliness in school but still litters his room with toys, you would agree that he has not applied the knowledge to his daily life. The assertion might not be accurate if he keeps a clean room in the first week of learning but fails to continue after the following weeks. It is not because of failed memory; it is due to a lack of desire, drive, and motivation to persist. We can generally say that he is not disciplined enough to continue.

Self-discipline entails every effort to control yourself. This definition might sound vague as you feel that you have always been in charge of your decisions. It might be correct, but what about your impulses, emotions, and feelings? Those are the big cards of your successes and failures, depending on how well you have mastered the game. The ability to consciously commit yourself to fulfill your goals irrespective of varying feelings can be termed self-discipline.

By now, you must have improved your level of focus. Sustaining this achievement is why self-discipline is necessary as this will form another habit in you. The process will not be a fast one but will surely help your productivity level and sustain any of your learned positive behavior.

It will begin with a steady approach to carefully analyze what you do in line with becoming better. For example, trying the conscious listening exercise will allow you to adapt to the changing conditions of different sounds in your environment, and allows you to flow with the circumstance without affecting your mindfulness (inner self).

An acute understanding of this subject will help you to achieve an excellent result to maintain a top-notch focus, beat laziness, and defeat procrastination. Take to heart the following nuggets to sustained self-discipline:

1. Identify and Analyze your Triggers

Positioning yourself in a safe zone is not only necessary when involved in a hazardous task; it should be natural. Our helmet here is to sustain self-discipline is to identify the triggers that cause distraction. This action is not only aimed at achieving success alone but digging deep to the root to measure the cause of its repeated failure. What causes you to lose focus? What are those factors that push you to perform the task in the future?

Do a proper assessment of those elements and be sincere as much as possible. The same thing goes to those triggers that increase your productivity level. It is possible to have the same factor contributing to both increased productivity and procrastination. For example, your partner at your workplace might inspire you to do more through his unrelenting attitude to work, and at the same time, make you an addict to the digital world.

Once you are clear on your triggers, propose alternative options to scale through. Try to write them down. It may involve the same way you write your to-do-list. Create another not-to-do-list to counter those issues. Through this approach, you won't see yourself falling into the same pit time and again.

2.   Be Sure of Your Purpose

A strong desire to win will be required to maintain an unwavering self-discipline course. Ask a series of questions. Why do I want to read a chapter of a book a day? Why must I eat cereal once in every two days? Self-awareness is necessary to keep you going. Analyze your feelings and emotions to be sure that you are not playing on them. Have a clarity that your pre-learned behavior is not on a temporary assumption or influenced by the rhythm of the moment.

3.   Build a Motivation Block

Create a system that will continuously fuel your passion to commitment. It might be a competitive environment where you can outwork or outperform others. Since you can measure your progress with hardworking colleagues, your progress will be on track.

Another motivation block can be to introduce a reward-and-punishment tool. The reward tool might be to buy an item for yourself every time you achieve or surpass a target. It might also be to take a time-out to have fun. You might think of paying a friend an agreed sum of money as your punishment tool. Just ensure that your motivation is keeping you going.

4. Choose a Model

Look to the outside world to keep on track. Search for someone who has been on the path you want to tread. He/she should be someone who has mastered the habit and have proven to develop over time. He might be your college professor, your gym instructor, or your spiritual head. Be sure you are right on whom to choose. Get ready to follow whatever you are told to do. It might look rigorous at first, but the desired outcome will surface.

5. Design a Strategy

Here is one of the essential tools to maintain self-discipline: Develop a plan to work with. Discipline is not automatic as it involves a process of building. Your action must comprise of a deadline and an achievable step-to-step guide. The good thing about these mini milestones is that you will be able to measure your progress. And a sound reward system can keep you focused and master an active control system.

The aim of this plan is not to get overwhelmed by your goals. Progress is the primary fuel that will push you farther to actualize your strategies. Deadlines also will force you to gather all resources at your reach to achieve success on a specific date.

Chapter Five: Goal Setting For Success

You may have spent a lot of time wondering why things don't just seem to work out well for you. One time you have a dream burning in your mind with full plans to accomplish that dream, and the next thing you know, it is gone, and you have accomplished nothing. You may have also spent a lot of time in thoughts, comparing yourself with people who achieve things with ease; people who it seems were simply born to be successful. These people know what they want, state what they want, and follow it with all their zeal until they see it achieved.

There is little or no secret attached to these people and their success. The only thing that differentiates you from them is the ability to set goals. These people don't only work hard; they work smart. And working smart entails setting strong and workable goals. Without goals, life would simply be directionless, and a directionless life will be an unproductive life with nothing to live for.

Most of the time, only a few of us sit down and chart a course for our lives. Take life like a stormy sea, with you and your boat floating on that sea. There is every possibility of you being taken off course. But if you have a compass, it will be easier for you to find your way home after the storm has subsided. Your goal is like a compass that helps to put you back in check after a period of going astray.

In this chapter, we will be going through some of the basics of setting goals. What are the best techniques and tips that you should employ while setting goals? How realistic and workable should your goals be so that they don't end up frustrating you as you work towards achieving them?

Concepts Associated with Goal Setting

Before we begin to explore the necessary techniques for goal setting, there are some concepts about goal setting that you have to understand. If these are not well-understood, then I tell you that the whole process will end up filled with failure. The most important question of all is:

Why do I need to set goals? This is a very personal question, and you would need to provide a personal answer before you can go on. Without providing an answer, you will never be able to connect with the goal-setting activity on a more personal level.

In setting goals, these two things will help you out in forging something that works.

- **What are your goals?** What exactly is it that you want? Do you want to land on the moon someday? Do you need to lose more than 100 pounds with 6 months? Are you planning to win an Oscar before you turn 40? Identify these goals because they will provide you with instant clarity. The goals will help your mind as a compass to accomplishment. In fact, an identified goal sets your heart on fire like no other.
- **Why do you want to accomplish these goals?** I can't tell you anything more important in goal setting. Without a purpose or a reason, your goals are as good as nuts. Take some time off and evaluate your reason for setting these goals? Do you need to get a good car so it would help you feel good around your peers or because it will help you move faster around town? Are you trying to lose weight because someone insulted you about your plus-size or because you simply want to live healthier? As you may know, a goal set for a selfish reason never gets to see the light of day as regards its achievement. With a concrete and well-laid purpose, your goal setting will be a whole lot more easily.

Forms of Goals

To effectively set a goal, you need to understand what kind of goal you are setting. There are different types and finding the right one will help you a long way. The most important form of goal categorization is the one that is done based on the timeline. These include:

1. **Short-Term Goals:** These goals are those that can be achieved in a short time, say within a period of six months or less than a year. When setting such goals, you should look at those that can be easily achieved so that you can go forward with the next goal.
2. **Long-Term Goals:** These goals take a longer space of time before they fully actualized. They even take years. Some of these goals make include learning and starting up a business, raising a child, or beating cancer.
3. **Lifelong Goals:** Goals like these may take you a lifetime to accomplish. The thing with lifelong goals is that you may never know when they will be accomplished. At some point, you are bound to get frustrated and want to give up. But you should note that lifelong goals as built on the achievement of long-term and short-term goals. A goal example of a lifelong goal is a child with a dream of becoming the President.

10 Goal-Setting Techniques to Achieve your Goals Faster

1. **Identify the Benefits of Achieving that Goal.**

It is one thing for you to know the purpose of following a goal through to the end, and it is a different thing to understand the benefit of achieving that goal. If a goal comes with no benefit, either for you or the people around you, then there will be no need to pursue it because even your mind will feel frustrated trying to compel you to action.

Knowing what is in it for you will be enough drive to help you sit up and get to work. For an exercise, pick your goal-setting book and jot down some of the benefits that you will enjoy if a goal is achieved. Think long and hard while filling those spaces with answers.

2. Set Compatible Goals.

When trying to set goals you can easily achieve, it is necessary that you make them compatible with each other. Setting incompatible goals make you waste your time and energy. Soon you will find yourself feeling very stressed out and weak, unable to go on with the pursuit of your goals. One goal may be to spend more time with people and make new friends, and another goal may be to learn how to be on your own more often and focus on a given task. These two are conflicting. You can't spend more time with friends and still have enough time to complete the task. When putting down goals, it is necessary that you look into each of them and measure their compatibility with the rest of them on the list.

3. Create a Standing Balance.

Don't allow yourself to get too involved in trying to achieve a particular goal that you begin to ignore the others. Life works with balance. You should learn to share your time equally amongst all of your goals. It will make no sense that you succeed in one aspect and fail in the other. You might be experiencing a lot of success in one aspect of your life, but when you discover that the other aspect is unfinished, it might be too late.

4. Ask for Help When Necessary.

That is why they are called goals; you can't achieve them alone. There are a lot of people around you who will be willing to help you out with your goals if only you will agree to be humble and meet them. For every goal you may want to achieve, there is someone out there who has achieved that goal a long time ago. You should connect with them and find out how they did it, what obstacles they faced, and how they overcame.

When analyzing your goals, try to identify places in which you can be helped so that you will be more specific in seeking that help. These can include skills you make need to acquire or knowledge to be gotten.

5. Focus on the Things that will Enhance your Goals.

When making your schedule for the day, try to basically consider those things that will add value to your goals. Those are the things that you should consider the most. They should take up more of your time. There are other activities that you can modify to help you create more time for these other activities. Do not hesitate to do those.

6. There is Work to be Done, and No One will Help you Do it.

This is probably the most important thing you should know about goal setting. It is not just about writing down the goals in a book and staring at them all day long. There is a lot more attached to it, and most of it is work. You should learn to take up the responsibility that will be associated with the work that you are about to do. At some points, if you begin to experience failure, your mind will be eager to help you shift blame. Please overcome this pleasurable temptation. It will lead you nowhere tangible. Instead of allowing yourself to get trapped in the web of complaints and excuses, make up your mind that no matter what happens, that goal must be accomplished.

7. Do Away with Potential Interruptions and Distractions

You will encounter a lot of distractions and interruptions on your way to achieving your goals. They will come in many disguises, and parade themselves as things that need to be accomplished urgently. Perhaps some of them might be legit, so you would need you the discretion to be able to select the wheat from the tares. Most of them will simply be time wasters on a mission to kill your time and slow you down. The ability to successfully differentiate which activities are worth your time is a very important skill you will need to master if you must accomplish those goals.

8. Stay Open to Change

A lot of unexpected things can arise, and you may need to make some changes to your goals. It may be a positive change, but a change all the same. Once you notice that something unplanned and unforeseen is about to take place, that will be the perfect time to make evaluations and know those things that can be changed. You can also keep your mind open and look for opportunities in them.

9. You Will Need a Level of Persistence

Working towards your goal is not all you may need to do to get them to achieve. Putting in all the required effort at the initial stage and then faltering at the end will only make you regret the whole process. Persistence is the necessary spice that makes your hard work pay off. You will surely meet a lot of hard bumps on your way but keeping up with everything required of you is something that will guarantee you success in the long run. Remember that all the things you will be doing now will only be short-term sacrifices, and they will provide you with long-term pleasures. It is up to you.

10. Constantly Review your Goals

Reviewing your goal will help you to identify any progress you may have made over time. It also provides you with the opportunity to pinpoint the places where you may have failed. When reviewing your goals, ask yourself questions about how far you have come achieving the goal, what steps should be changed towards achieving the goal with more speed and if you are still on the right track. Goal review will also help you motivate you towards performing better.

7 Things you Need to Know About Setting the Right Goals

I always tell my audience to find the right goals to set. There are goals for you, and then there are goals that you shouldn't bother setting because they will yield no value to your life. If the right goals are not being set, then there is every possibility of you losing focus even before they are accomplished. Setting the right goals will take some time. The right goals don't just come to you prepared. You might need to brainstorm some ideas before you find which goals are right for you and which aren't. But there are some general techniques you can put in place to help you with your selection. Here are some of them:

1. **The Right Goal can be Measured**

Your goals should be goals that can be easily measured to find out how successful you have been with them. If you write down your goals and break them into bits, then there should be an avenue for you to be able to tick them and measure success. A goal that can be measured should be one that is specific, like, "I will lose ten pounds before the months runs out." or "I should finish writing my next book before the year runs out." All of these are examples of measurable goals. These kinds of goals make it easy for you to track success.

2. **The Right Goals can be Managed**

If you find yourself constantly being overwhelmed by a goal, it may mean that it is not the right goal for you. The right goal is that goal that you can break down into smaller goals. These smaller goals will serve as milestones that will build up to the accomplishment of the main goal. Breaking your goals into smaller bits will help you keep track of its success rate.

3. **The Right Goal can be Achieved No Matter the Hurdles that Come with it**

Each goal on your goal list must have a point with which you can finally measure success. If your goal does have that point where you can look back and say you have come a long way, then it is an abstract goal. Setting a goal and saying, "I want to sell my products" is not a goal. How many of those products do you want to sell? If you don't clearly define what an achievement is for you, then you won't be able to reward yourself even when you sell a thousand of those products. In your mind, the goal remains unachieved, and soon, you will give up on it. The main thing is to place a target on all your goals.

4. **Any Obstacles Against the Accomplishment of the Right Goals can Easily be Detected a Long Way Off**

If you run into unforeseen problems while trying to execute a goal, you can take that as a point that the goal wasn't meant for you all along. The right goal is one that allows you to detect any future problems while you are making a review of the steps required to accomplish it. Once these problems present themselves in the initial stage, all you have to do is put in measures to mitigate their effect.

5. **The Right Goal will have a realistic and workable deadline**

Every goal needs a timeframe, a period with which it should be accomplished. With a set deadline, your mind is moved to work to produce a result. Once you have come up with a timeframe within which your job should be accomplished, you will find out that a sense of urgency will be instantly attached to the job. And having a sense of urgency is something I mentioned earlier, which will help you with your goal-setting venture. There should be enough time that will help you reach the goal, yet the time shouldn't be too long to get you uninterested in the goal. But you should put the magnitude of your goal into consideration when setting a timeframe, so you don't end up deceiving yourself.

6. The Right Goal can be Easily Visualized

If you don't have a picture, then you don't have a destination. Does our goal give you a picture? If it does, how tangible and real, is it? When making a review of your goals, picture yourself accomplishing the goal. Picture yourself holding your complete novel in your hands. Picture yourself with your degree in three years' time. Picture yourself in your car. The stronger and clearer the picture, the easier it will be to get the motivation to work towards it. You can easily rejuvenate a dull and unmotivated day by imagining the results of your success. Your goals must have a picture.

7. The Right Goal will Always Have a Long-Term Value for your Life

Finally, the right goal is a goal that has rewards that will stay with you for a lifetime. Although there are the right goals with short-lived rewards, most of the right goals always come with rewards that stay longer. When setting each goal, try to analyze and identify the benefits associated with each of them. They may include financial freedom, mental rest, physical health, and psychological stability. Whatever they may be, just know that identifying them will help you a long way.

The Best Ways to Reward Yourself for Completed Goals

First, you have to understand that no one will reward you more than you can reward yourself. You deserve to be rewarded, especially when you have successfully completed a task, herculean or not. Reward your body. Reward your mind. Reward your soul. Reward yourself no matter how little it may be. It definitely goes a long way. To reward yourself is to tell your mind and brain that it has done a good job and will encourage it to do more. Once you can establish this in your mind, you will find out that it will be a lot easier for you to work because your body will be looking forward to that reward received after the first completed job.

To start the process of rewarding yourself, you have to know what the reward will be for. Take out a pen and book and jot down whatever you may want to reward yourself for. Make sure that you have a detailed and comprehensive list before going ahead with the rewarding process. If not, you will only be deceiving yourself. There are many ways for you to reward yourself, and I will introduce you to some of them. But you should also note that your rewards should not come in such a way that they will negate everything you have just worked for. That will be the wrong reward system. The most important things to consider when selecting reward are:

1.   It Should Have Long-Lasting Value
The reward should be of value to you in any way possible. Don't just go for a reward that will provide you with instant happiness; go for something more concrete and deep. Look for a reward that will gratify even your soul. You can go for a spiritual experience and see life in a whole new way.

The core of your selection should be of self-compassion. Be kind to yourself, because of the benefits of self-kindness are numerous and overwhelming. It should not be a one-time reward but should be practiced as much as possible whenever a task is completed.

2. It Infuses Positivity

Your rewards should also drive you towards accomplishing more than you have achieved before. Acknowledge of all of the things that you have achieved now but strive to do more in no time. Your reward should remind you about the importance of not being too hard on yourself.

3. There Should be a Necessary Balance in the Reward System

Don't allow your reward system to go over the top. There has to be a sensible balance. The reward should not exceed the size of the completed tasks that necessitated them.

4. Tone it Down

Sometimes your reward can come from within you, just something inside of you. It can just be a quiet day or moment when you sit and reflect everything on your journey. That can be a clear moment of enlightenment that will assist you in your future journey.

5. You don't have to spend a lot to reward yourself.

Rewards can simply be the things you enjoy doing.

6. It should be easy to achieve as fast as possible.

No More Procrastination

Here are some quick ways in which you can reward yourself after completing a task. There is a wide variety, and it is up to you to choose the one that suits you.

1. Go to a concert.
2. Visit a carnival or a music festival.
3. Go see a movie with some friends.
4. Listen to a captivation podcast.
5. Plan a night out with family members.
6. Enjoy a magazine read with a glass of cold juice.
7. Soak your body in a hot bath in the bathtub.
8. Stream some danceable music online.
9. Stream some interesting documentaries on Netflix.
10. Go for a long walk in your favorite park.
11. Join an exercise or dance class.
12. Visit an art gallery and see inspiring artwork.
13. Treat yourself to a foreign meal.
14. Visit a spa and get a royal treatment.
15. Have a picnic at a nearby beach.
16. Attend a sports event and cheer your favorite team.
17. Have a small get-together and celebrate with your friends.
18. Engage your hands in an art form that you love or in gardening.
19. Reorganize your room and closet.
20. Take photos of yourself.
21. Get a new hairdo.
22. Have a free day where you lie around, doing what you want or doing nothing at all. (But don't allow the pleasure of such a day get into your head. Once the day is over you go back to your routine.)
23. Write a short story about yourself and share it on social media.
24. Buy a new perfume with a fragrance that you love.
25. Get yourself some new clothes and discard off some old ones. Or you can give them out too.

26. Travel to a place you have always wanted to travel to.

Chapter Six: New You, New Routines

Growth in itself is the influence of greatness and achievement. Life has taught us to improve on everything, even the most common of things. Human beings are not separate from becoming better. We have come to learn the hard way through trial and error. And for this, history has related the importance of self-growth and the attitude needed to attain this level of excellence.

From the values required to the skills and knowledge needed, all these virtues can be learned. And the truth lies in the opportunity life has presented to learn continuously. The more we see the need to adopt new techniques and learn skills, the more comfortable living becomes. And since we don't live in isolation, the people around us get motivated through our process of learning. For example, renowned leaders invest a great time in knowledge and research; for that's one of the ways to break through to attainment.

Learning comes with many hurdles to climb, and no one says it's easy to adopt a new behavior. The fuel to sustain this change mostly comes from proven structures. One of them has to do with you. It is a positive attitude to see beyond your immediate mindset and embrace the newness you have seen people become. Once your mind is open, every other thing that relates to tranquility, togetherness, goal setting, and discipline will be natural to you. Your mind will now become fertile ground for breeding positive habits. You would be able to think brightly and expect the best to happen always.

A new routine begins with a firm conviction to do things differently. You might be tired of the results you make per time, and you feel something is missing. You are correct! If you have been thinking in this direction, then, you are ready to make an impact. This level is the foundation of your success. It is now evident that you are prepared to stand out without losing your uniqueness.

Don't be overwhelmed with the desire to get great results; it is attainable. But you need to understand that it is not automatic. The process involved needs you to review your choices creatively. You might also need to break down your preferences, emotions, and thought patterns to sooth the new routine you have chosen. Be sure that trends do not influence your choice to do things differently. Trends are like fashion; they come and vanish with time.

8 Ways to Create Great Habits that Lead to Success

The undeniable truth about success is that it has to be maintained. Sustaining excellence, achievement, and productivity starts with the most ignored principle. This standard is what I call the "principle of continuous growth." It deals with a conscious effort to regularly checkmate human composition to become better. Checkmating here means consistent appraisal of our emotions, skills, abilities, values, and attitudes to fit into the intended learning process. You need to ask questions to look for solutions instead of dwelling on the adverse reports.

How humans spend time goes a long way in accounting for productivity. The attitude put to the time also has a significant effect on whether the moment is valid or not. Certain elements might have acclimatized themselves to our views, making us prone to its negative impact. Such properties become our daily reference, disposition, belief, assumption, perception, and doctrine. Those are what result in habit, and we unconsciously repeat the pattern in our daily lives. The excellent news about a habit is that it can be learned. Your awareness of this routine and willingness to change is what matters most. I will outline below some great patterns that will inspire you to a successful life.

1. Identify the Kind of Routine you Want.

When a destination is known, the path to get there will be quite straightforward. See to it that you have convinced yourself of the kind of habit you want to break. This realization should be what matters most to you at the moment; a top priority that should not be postponed. Engage this decision in your thoughts consistently, but don't get carried away.

Identifying a negative habit is great; positioning your mind to replace it with a positive one will be more fulfilling. Satisfy your conscience and willpower to get set on the new journey of an improved person. It is necessary to be inwardly persuaded because that is the fuel that keeps the consistency going.

This stage of identification needs a proper breakdown of your engagement. Let's start with the little things that keep you busy like gossip. You need to know when and how the chat starts if your new routine is to get focused on writing a 1000-word report on safety per day every time you close from work. Then shut down any signal that suggests a delay in time and mental capabilities. While it might have been a frequent occurrence to chat at the parking lot, decide to shorten the discussion when you notice it's going south. You are in charge here, and that's the reason you need to be sincere. This is just an example, and yours might be different.

Also, realize that you will be in charge of your activities since you could predict what you desire. No one forced you into it; it's a personal choice so that mindfulness will set in. You would be able to position yourself to the present target and not get overwhelmed with the uncertainties of the future.

With the awareness of the present, you will be able to channel your energy and resources to achieving a present task. It will be more comfortable to accept the feelings and thoughts pattern that follows awareness.

Knowing what you want to achieve now and in the future places you on what it takes to attain them. Sacrifice is top of them. The newly identified routine is most likely not to follow your conventional way of life. And if yours is completely different, then get ready to adapt to the changes. Your time on the social network might need to change and hangout moments will adjust. Whatever it is you feel will be affected, prepare for it so as not to cause a delay along the path of successful attainment.

2.   Start From your Current Position.

It might sound ridiculous when you see yourself not going at a fast pace. But the truth is, that is the perfect pace for you. Remember that habit constitutes a whole part of us, and the significant change won't come as quick as you imagine. The will to move is the necessary speed you need here.

Think of it as like building your muscles. You should know that the physical build-up won't surface in a day. You might be longing to stick to reading for three hours every evening. Understand that you would have used most of your productive moments during the day, and the possibility of reading at a stretch is slim since you are starting new. Why not start with thirty minutes and master the art for the first two weeks. Once you are consistent with the half an hour routine, increase the duration progressively. Ensure that you have established the behavior, and then seek to maintain it.

3.   Recreate your Surroundings.

You are not the perfect composition of yourself without your environment. Some triggers stabilize your old habit, and most of them are within your reach. First, identify what they are and how they start. Those triggers might not signal delay and procrastination, but in the real sense, they are the villain.

Your new habit might be to start a new diet, but it seems your kitchen is still stuck with your old meals. It will be best to remove those foods or probably don't shop for them. It will be hard to focus on your new routine because the more you see those foods around, the harder it becomes to do away with them.

Reorganize your house, office, table, and even wardrobe to suit your expected behavior. The more you clear off distractions, the better your chance of success. The idea here is to get rid of the energy that makes learning difficult for you and replace it with good ones.

4.   Move with People that Encourage you.

Your motivation for sticking to a learned behavior will be boosted when you are accountable to your friends. It is not compulsory to report to your acquaintance. It might be a colleague at work or your mentor. Choose someone you trust enough to criticize your report.

Your focus at this point is that you are not on the path of newness alone; there are external bodies that support your new habit. You will achieve optimum results if you choose someone successful in learning your selected routine. This way, he will be able to guide you constructively.

The significant result you want to see in the new routine can also be fostered when you see it as teamwork. Imagine your clique deciding to start a new habit. Every one of you will be motivated to put in your best. One good thing you will keep in mind is that "there is someone next to me I can always refer to," and he/she will be your most active encouragement. It will be difficult for you to stop. You might decide to speak your friends into learning a new behavior to enhance a fast rate of the result.

5. Tell Others about your Plan.

Most people are scared of failure, and failure in itself is an ailment that can be avoided. A better way humans prevent it is by pushing their energy to succeed. Think of yourself as someone that can be trusted with information. Confidentiality is not the highlight here but openness and accountability; knowing that a piece of you has been pre-committed to someone else. You will have to stick to your habit as a matter of necessity because you won't want to disappoint them.

You might start by informing some of your followers on social networks, friends, family members, and colleagues. Tell them beforehand and continuously engage them in your commitment routine. You might not want to disappoint them by backing off. Each time you face the temptation of going back, it's most likely to remember those you have pledged to.

6. Work Out your New Habit in the Line of the Old.

The energy involved in learning a new pattern is quite different from the complacent comfort of the old one. You will agree that the old routine would have gained access-control over you. Your life would have been repositioned to think and work in that direction. Telling you to dump the old habit immediately will be like asking you to change your skin color thrice a week. It is best to adjust your new behavior with the old one. Remember our first point to start small.

Since you have a plan already, make your strategy as flexible as possible. Be careful here as not to fall prey to negative thoughts. Your tendencies to flow with your daily experience will remind you of negativity, replace them with positive affirmations. As much as you commit to the new behavior steadily, you will get to become better and progress to become a different person.

7. Reward Every Stage of Progress.

Take note of your progress and commend every fulfillment of your desired results. No one can encourage you better than yourself. Reward here should not force you to remain on the spot. If you feel that you have not been motivated to do more while applauding yourself, change how you apply it. Create a conditional reward system. Watch the movie after you have finished off the report. Enjoy the evening with your clique whenever your room is perfectly clean. You can go with the flow of your reward after you have achieved your targets.

8. Engage in Mental Exercise

Your brain is not isolated from your new routine. Your cognitive capabilities have a significant role to play after your willpower. Start with your regular exercise, which might be walking around the park or jogging. While doing any of those exercises, think of the new habits you want to create. Allow your brain to process the information into consciousness, but don't get overwhelmed. This state of knowledge allows you to come into the present realities all the time. You will now be able to avoid distractions because your brain has processed your new routine into its system.

Remember that every makeup of your body matters, and your brain shouldn't be left out. You might also consider doing the exercises that sharpen focus given in this book.

9 Morning Routine to Make Every Day a Good Day

Nature has loaded a bountiful pack of benefits to the early hours of the day. And you will agree that creativity and innovation tend to flow freely during this time. Although this varies from the kind of person you are, it still does not negate how productivity can be achieved. This section will provide activities to perform to maximize your morning. Following them promptly will set the tone for an excellent day.

1.   Make a Journal of your Thoughts and Use it for your Day.

The refreshing times of the morning are the best moment to write down what comes to your mind. Every one of your activities during the day might defer you the privilege, and that's why you must maximize the opportunity the early hours give.

Note that you might not need to do this brief exercise the conventional way. Be flexible enough to go with the flow of your thoughts. It might only involve ten minutes of your time. The bright side of journaling your opinion is that your brain is connected to a source of mindfulness. You won't need to stress your cognitive capability to remember the little things that flood your heart. Now you will be conscious of every idea that would boost your daily experience.

If you will need to create an outline of your thoughts, list them out! You may want to replicate writing the results of daily views. This action will make you reference your success story and remind you of your previous wins. You would also be able to repeat the same routine that brings achievement the next time you face a seemingly related challenge.

2. Fix your Bed

Does it sound a bit stressing? Yes! Because you have not been practicing it. This simple homemaking skill gives you a sense of responsibility for yourself. Your bed has been able to create the first task of the day successfully. Prove to yourself how successful you want this to be. Every time you do this excellently well, you build a sense of fulfillment.

3. Don't Conclude on Essential Decisions

Instinct might have guided you before now, but reality is not a game of chance; it will surely play out its rule. Leave your thoughts on the paper and get to finalize them later in the day. Most times, the inner will to make a perfect decision might not be strong enough to give an accurate strategy needed in achieving your goals. Be patient enough to research your perceived inspiration. Your search throughout the day will enhance better mental productivity for the subsequent mornings.

4. Limit your Choices

This early period of the day forces you to make the inevitable choice for your day. Streamline your selection to your set of values. You might be bugged with the color, type of shirt, shoe, and gown to wear.

The accessories to use might even eat up a lot of your thinking time. Create a routine of your basic needs in the morning and make it practicable. For example, wake up, meditate, choose my clothing, bathe, make coffee, organize, and get set for the day. Simplify your daily choices, and don't make it grievous for yourself.

5. **Energize your Body**

Think of fitness as another tool to maintain a morning routine. You might not need to go jogging down the street. Your room can allow you to sweat out the energy required for the day. Remember the conditional method of reward you read under creating a habit that leads to success? Make it work for you here also.

Do 15 to 30 push-ups, after which you consider reviewing your activities for the day. You may also want to outstretch your arms and legs and then think about the day's task. Going through those exercises would have prepared your body for the job of the day. Your mind now will be at rest, and your happiness level is increased for the rest of the day.

6. **Affirmations**

Positive thinking, they say, result in a positive result. Create a mind full of positivity as you make affirmations that will reframe your mind. You often see through your mind; making it a necessity to flush out negativity for the day. Remember, it requires self-talk. Take out time to write your affirmations and read it to yourself. You may start with the simple challenge you had the day before and make good out of it. For example, say, "I walked with excellence today." "I achieved and surpassed targets today." "I am not overwhelmed with success or failure. I excel in my entire task."

7. **Focus More on your Inner Self**

The strength received from meditation can be enough to pull one through the mental challenges of the day. You will achieve this level of calmness when you separate yourself from both external and inward attachment. Create the willingness to break from the outer world for the moment. Breaking here means creating a focus on yourself, especially your willpower.

Note that this simple exercise requires you to clear off every thought and worry. Your anxiety level must be consciously reduced at this period. Look only at yourself, and not even at social networks. Plan to achieve this rare routine from your evening. No early checking of emails, Facebook, and blogs. Just you alone.

Disassociate yourself from your daily routine of dullness and inactiveness for this brief period in the morning. A 15-minute moment of reflection is a good start for you. See the possibility of attaining success for the day. Reflect on the affirmations you have made and see yourself achieving them. You are feeding your soul at this point to have a winning mindset. And that's how best to describe your day for anyone.

8. Try a Cold Shower

You might not be comfortable with this for the first time. But you can try it a few times and make a habit of it intermittently. Think of the advantages it comes with. Your blood flow tends to increase and makes you active for the day. You would be brave to start and doing this releases dopamine into your body. Your body is then left with the feeling of activeness, motivation, and pleasure. The bath will be an excellent icing to design the day.

9. Plan for a Healthy Breakfast

Understand the healthiness of feeding in the morning. It is essential to combine certain nutrients like protein, minerals, and vitamins together to have a great appetite and to fulfill nutritional needs. Although other nutrients are also necessary, healthy fats and proteins help stabilize your emotions. Remember that your mood needs to be right. Take, for example, a fiber-rich toast and topping. The fiber in this food helps slow digestion, enhancing stable blood sugar. Think of other simple but healthy meals for your breakfast.

6 Evening Routines to Ensure Tomorrow is just as Good as Today.

The best day results from a well-planned evening. Opportunities are loaded in the evening when you take up the challenge to be responsive. Understand what you need to do right before going to bed. Those activities will make up your evening routines. I know that your day might have made you weary, but you can readjust your mood and mental activeness. You can make your rest a blissful experience.

1. **Reflect on your Day.**

What happened at work today? Why was I issued a query letter? Ask many questions as possible. You deserve to know what has taken up your entire day. Use this period to identify the cause of your actions. Why did I react badly to a customer? Why was I angry during the lunch break? Don't stop with asking questions; break your query down to triggers. See what makes you do a particular thing.

Reflection doesn't mean you should use this period to think of your inadequacies alone. You might want to think of your targets that you met or surpassed. Do a proper assessment of your day's activities to know what goals to set for the other days.

2. **Make a List of your Goals.**

Look into the future of productivity and plan what you desire to attain. This process must be intentional because you might not have analyzed the challenges of the day. Design another structure to help you achieve more. Give a proper definition to your destination. Ensure that you eliminate rigidity in your approach to take in the future. After you have drafted out your goals, paste it where you could easily see it. It could be on your reading table or at the back of your door. Build an assurance that you are set for the following morning. Plan for your breakfast, your choice of clothes, and your time to wake up. It might take some time to get ready if you are doing it for the first time. Consistency in setting goals for the next day result in becoming an active organizer in the long run. Waking up to this reality helps you set your mind on attaining targets.

You may also want to read your goals to yourself. Just as you recite your affirmations, your attention in doing this is to activate mindfulness. Live in the reality of having your goals in your mind

3.   **Take Time to Read.**

Engage your mind in learning something new! Doing this will get you ready for the following day. You might not need to do the long hours as you might be tired of the day's work. You might want to use this period to develop ideas you have written down in the morning. Research also on your challenge at work and learn from the experience of professionals.

4.   **Read up Affirmations.**

Just like how you began your day with words of positivity, you might consider ending your day with it as well. Since you have reflected and analyzed the happenings of the day, use your conclusion to say beautiful things to your consciousness. You may say, "I was not overwhelmed because of failure." "I achieved better than I did today."

"I see myself attaining my career goals." "My tomorrow is active and vibrant, and I stay happy with my friends and colleagues." Design your affirmations to suit your value.

5. Chat with your Family.

Bonding together as a family is an excellent ritual to practice. Take time out to say personal things to your spouse and children. And if you are single or living alone, find a means of communicating with your family. Every part of your discussion here should center on the family needs. Find out what your daughter desires of you. Inform her also of what you require of her to become successful in life. You might not want to do the job of a life coach every night, but ensure you build intimacy with your family. Also, engage your spouse in an intimate discussion. You may seek ideas relating to your work schedules and pattern.

6. Don't Give in to Idleness.

Setting yourself up for what to do does not mean doing anything, it means doing a specific task. Think of a job that will boost your mental alertness. Reading, meditation, exercise, cooking, etc. may be an excellent task to perform. Avoid the trap of getting caught up in a massive job for the evening. The blue screen should be a thing to avoid at this time.

Since you need to start small, you may also think of fixing your clutter. Arrange the pile of books on the table and clear your wardrobe.

Chapter Seven: No More Obstacles

7 Ways to Conquer Your Fear of Failure

It is natural to fear. It is one of the things that make us human. Fear will always present itself whenever you are about to embark on a brand-new venture. Yet fear, too, can be very dangerous. It can hold you back from accomplishing what you need to accomplish.

Fear can manifest itself in a lot of ways. There is the fear of heights, the fear of rising water, and the fear of spiders, and so on. But as regards being productive, the fear that relates to us the most is the fear of failure.

Failure is absolutely nothing to be afraid of. Even the richest, the most powerful, and the most successful amongst us have once experienced failure at one point in time or another. So, if you ever fail, you should know that you are not alone. You will get through it.

It is just like falling sick. People put in a lot of measures in place so that they don't fall sick. Unfortunately, no matter how much they try, they ultimately fall sick one day. What do you do in that situation? You don't run away from sickness; you fight it. And once it leaves you, your body learns and adapts so that the next time there is an attack from that pathogen, it will know how to react and protect you.

The same goes for your failure. Learn from it. Build your stamina from it. When it first hits you, it will seem like your world is about to crumble to pieces, but I assure you that it will only be for a moment. These tips will help you manage and overcome the fear of failure:

1. **Stand Up to it.**

Life is a battleground. If you are not ready to fight, then get ready to live a miserable life. Nothing will ever be handed over to you on a platter of gold, except if your family has stacks of gold bars somewhere in the World Bank. To see success, to have accomplishments, you should know that you will have to stand up to your fear of failure. The fear of failure is not failure itself, but it is a strong pathway that leads towards failure. The best you can do for yourself is to push yourself out of that pathway into the pathway of success.

2. **Show yourself some Kindness.**

Don't beat yourself down. Don't be too harsh on yourself. Understand that the fear you have for failure is something natural; but it doesn't mean that you are not good enough. Nobody is good enough; we are all striving to be better. So, don't beat yourself up simply because you did not hit the mark the first time. There are still a lot of open opportunities for you to try and be better.

3. **Understand that Failing Once does not Make you a Complete Failure.**

You only become a total failure when you decide to give and stop chasing. The point where you decide to give up becomes the point where your success story ends, so it all depends on you and how well you choose to maximize your strengths. A lot of successful figures that we look up to today once failed, but that didn't make them consider themselves failures. They kept up with the struggle and brought something admirable.

4. **Feed your Mind with Optimism.**

A lot of people experience failure every day, but that doesn't mean that you must be one of them. A thought will present itself and ask you,

"What if you fail?" I want you to challenge that thought by asking, "What if I succeed?" People fail, and people also succeed. It all depends on the group you decide to identify yourself with. If there is ever going to be a successful person in that field, then it could be you.

5. **Free yourself from the Obsession of Perfectionism**

Many people have been tied down because of the need to get it right the first time. You don't have to get it right the first time. Have that at the back of your mind. Nothing good that was ever created was perfect in one go. Accept the fact that you might not hit your target at first, but that does not mean that you will stop trying. The process of trying to perfect something is itself a learning process. As you keep on doing that, you will keep getting better at it until you become as good as you want to be.

6. **Why do you Fear Failure?**

For some people, the fear of failure stems from all the things they have heard about failure. Others just don't want others to see them as a failure. Hence, they begin to nurture fear for it. Whatever the case may be, try to find out the reason why you fear failure and do well to tackle it early. Are you afraid because you do not fully understand the task at hand? Then do well to understand it better. Are you afraid because you have heard scary stories of people who encountered failure? Then begin to put things in place that will help you overcome failure.

7. **Accept failure for what it is**

Failure is not a monster, nor is it a beast. It can only become as large as tormenting as you want it to be at any point in time. You define what your failure becomes for you. Seeing failure as something that will come and go, something that will come and pass, a fleeting moment in our lives, will help you to overcome your fear for it easily.

7 Strategies for Defeating the Monster of Perfectionism

To be perfect is an admirable quality, and a lot of people will die for that quality, to be free of any form of stain or blemish. Seeking to attain perfection will drive you towards producing work of high standards. To strive for perfection is not wrong in any way; in fact, it is quite necessary to produce work that will stand the test of time.

However, the pursuit of perfection can easily become an obsessive behavior if it is not left unchecked. People who pursue this are referred to as perfectionists, and most of the time, their standards are hardly ever met. This can, in turn, lead to a sort of frustration.

These perfectionists are never happy with anything until it meets their insanely high standards. Conversely, perfectionists seem always to want to put off some tasks simply because they are scared that they will never carry out that task well enough. This can somehow become a killer of productivity because such a person will never want to break into any new adventure and see what happens with it.

A piece of advice I always give to people is that they should learn to work with their perfectionism. Don't allow your high standards to hold you back from performing; instead make it work for you to produce a more admirable job. You do that by starting up the task. Drop your fear of imperfection and just start. Complete the task; and after completion, you can go back and add your touch of perfectionism to it.

The life of a perfectionist is quite boring because nothing new is ever explored. That shouldn't be the case with you. That is why you will need to get over your perfectionist mindset but not your high standards. Understand that perfection can never be attained, ever.

Instead, you can keep getting better and better. Here are some strategies you can employ to help you overcome perfectionism:

1. Learn to Accept When it is Good Enough When you have Put in your Whole Best.

Like I clearly stated, perfection is a myth. Even when you think you have achieved it, if you look closer, you will see that there are still flaws. You can literally drive yourself crazy. Try to understand when you have done enough in a particular project. Good is never enough, but your best can always suffice. Don't stress your mind. The best thing to do is to get into the flow and allow yourself to be moved ahead with it. You don't have to produce perfect work; all you have to do is produce your best work.

2. Understand that Perfectionism is a Time Killer

There are two major problems I have with perfectionists: the first is that they hardly ever start any task for fear of not producing to their standards. The second is that even when they begin a task, they spend a lot of time going through the steps, repeating them, just to produce a perfect job. The amount of time wasted is even enough to get them to ignore the job and get frustrated. No one is saying that you should not take your time. What I am saying is do not kill your time. These are two different concepts, and they mean different things. Take your time and give your the best. Know when to stop and leave the rest. There is only enough you can give to any project.

3. Understand that you can Hurt People with your Perfectionist Standards.

As has been pointed out before, never lower your standards, aim for the best quality, but not necessarily perfection. Perfection is unattainable. One thing about striving for perfection and high standards is that you are capable of hurting the people around you with your standards. Not everyone is like you. Not everyone is a perfectionist like you. Some people only want to put in their best into what they do, and that is all. When you continue to drop the weight of your unachievable standards on them, you can crush them and make them hate you. Nothing they will ever do will ever be enough for you, and this alone is capable of hurting your relationship with them. Make sure to get the best from your employees and workers at all times, but don't become a frustrating master that can never be pleased.

4. **Eliminate the Competitive Mindset.**

For a lot of perfectionists, their character stems from being the best at all times. They want no other person ever to be ahead of them, and it frustrates them when their plans don't go as intended. There is a kind of competition known as the healthy competition, and that is the kind of competition that you should strive towards. Subscribe to the competition that brings out the best in you instead of dragging you towards envy.

Another thing you should understand is that you are your own biggest competitor. All you have to do is develop on yesterday, build on the success you have had in the past. And come to think of it, if you were perfect yesterday, what do you want to do today. Life is an adventure, and perfectionism breaks that adventure. It hinders you from discovering treasures. So, stay free and keep your mind on your own self.

5. **Eliminate Perfectionism Triggers in your Life.**

This will involve looking into a lot of things. Sometimes the people in your life may also be some of the factors causing your obsession with perfectionism. Because they are perfectionists themselves, they will do everything in their power to seek the same from you. Don't buy into that. Perfectionism, as I have explained to you, is stressful. It is left for you to carry out an inner analysis and identify all those things that trigger perfectionism in your life. Quench them.

6. **Reevaluate your Standards**

Perfectionism is a result of excessively high standards. You need to check yourself so you don't wreck yourself. It is not normal to expect a 3-year-old to be able to spell five-letter words correctly without missing out on any letters. But a perfectionist doesn't care. They just want it to be done, and they will have no idea that they are hurting that child.

Ask yourself if your standards are unrealistically high. Once you identify the high standards, you can then tone them down so that everybody benefits from it. You can also ask people around you who will be willing to help you identify those standards that you have to work on.

7. **Allow Imperfection Sometimes.**

You don't always have to perfect. We live in an imperfect world, yet we all enjoy the world and don't want to leave. The truth is that you can do with some imperfection in your life. Leave the bedsheets rough and rumpled as you leave the house. Allow the kids to dress themselves up. Just challenge any perfectionist tendencies you may have and see what happens.

7 Ways in Which Positivity can Manifest Success

Positivity, as a trait, does not mean smiling all the time and always carrying a cheerful look. It is way more profound than that. Positivity really has to do with your overall perspective of life. It is all about what you make with whatever life gives you at the moment, either negative or positive. "When life throws lemons at you, you make lemonade" is one quote that adequately captures the essence of positivity.

Research has proven over time that people who are happier, people who have more positivity in their lives, generally end up more successful than those who do not buy into the message of positivity. Positivity has been linked to better performance and productivity in workplaces. The presence of positive emotions always makes the generation of wonderful ideas. Some major benefits of positivity include:

- **Better mental performance and sharper response to stimuli.** Positive people generally tend to have brains that perform better and produce better results. Their mind travels wider during a brainstorm session, and they can come up with a wide range of ideas for a project. Ultimately, this leads to being more creative and productive people.
- **People tend to get closer to those who already carry a lot of positivity in them.** Positivity in a relationship also helps to build a strong and lasting connection between the parties involved.
- **The health benefits associated with positivity are enormous.** In fact, positivity can cause a person to eat healthier because their minds are always sharp to point out the things they should not be taking into their system. Depression, which is a by-product of negative thinking, has been connected to overweight and junk feeding. A positive mindset will mean a lower heart rate, lower blood pressure, and lower stress. People who stay positive are also known to sleep better.

- **Positivity helps to build a psychology of confidence, boosted self-esteem, and bodily energy.** With such energy to expend, positive people achieve their goals quite faster than non-positive people.

With all of these benefits listed, you can now see that it is quite important that you develop a positive mindset that will fuel your success. The question now is how you can do that. These strategies will help you:

1. **Keep your Focus on all the Good Things in your Life.**

Nobody has it all beautiful for them. We all have our ups and downs, where we face a lot of challenges daily. But the question remains how do you allow those challenges to define you? Of course, you will face the door, but you will also face up. How well do you keep your gaze on the good things in your life? Remember that every single day comes with its own benefits, no matter how bad that day goes. Learn to focus on these benefits for as long as you can.

2. **Learn all the Lessons that Life Throws at you.**

As I have stated numerous times in this book, every failure you come across in your life is a lesson if only you will choose to learn from it. Failures are prone to breed negative thoughts in your mind. These include: "I am not good enough." "I will never be worth it." and "I won't make it." But remember that each time you stumble in the dark, your body learns of obstacles on that path and never makes the same mistake again. That is why you can walk into your room even with the light off and make your way to the switch without hitting your toes on the cabinet.

3.   Encourage Yourself.
No one can talk to you like you can talk to yourself. There is no better motivation than the one you give yourself. Wake up each morning, look at yourself in the mirror, and release transformative mantras into your day. There is something about the words we speak. They possess a very strong creative power that can go ahead and provide us with the best results. Some people use this power to produce very negative results for themselves because they are always talking about the bad in their lives. These thoughts have a way of building strongholds in your mind and control you. Never allow them to do that. Always be the one in control and dictate what comes into your life.

4.   Keep your Mind on the Things Happening in your Present.
The present is your now, your reality at this moment, the things that are currently happening in your life. Some people live their lives for the future, while others live in the past. But I tell you that the most important time to live for is now. Don't lose your existence while chasing other realities.

5.   Keep Positive People and Positivity Around you.
A wall of negative thoughts is always on the rise in our mind, and it totally depends on you to determine if it continues to rise or it crumbles to the ground. You can destroy any form of negative walls by surrounding yourself with positive people and positive things. All of these will assist you in choking down any negativity bridling up around you. Find most people and place them around your life. Talk to them as much as you can and try to learn from them. They have a way of affecting yours into positivity.

6.   **Focus on your Goals.**

Negative thoughts are a form of distraction that results because people aren't obsessed with reaching their goals. A mind that stays focused on achieving goals and being the best will never have time to nurture any form of negativity. Keep yourself productive at all times, and continue to focus on how you can achieve more and outdo yourself.

7.   **Practice Gratefulness.**

This is one of the greatest tools you can use to activate a positive mindset for success. When you continue to stay grateful and thankful for the things around you, you rarely have time to think about the negatives.

5 Empowering Mantras to Destroy Self-Sabotage and Start Getting Stuff Done.

Funny enough, there has always been this kind of mythological attachments to the word "mantra." It has suffered almost the same fate as "meditation," where someone thinks it can only apply to a Buddhist monk in Tibet or a witch sitting on the Himalayas. Most times, we don't even understand how powerful mantras are and how they can help us generally.

What exactly is a mantra if you should use it? Take it this way: a mantra is a mind tool or a word, sentence, or sound that is used to keep your mind in place and prevent it from wandering off into distraction. Mantras can help you out in different facets of our life if they are employed in the right way. They can help you become more productive. They can help you to stay focused. They can help you to reframe your mind and the thoughts that swirl in it. The possibilities are endless, and that is why it is necessary that you begin to employ mantras in these different facets of your life so that you have the best of it. Here are some mantras that can help you overcome yourself and start getting stuff done.

1. **I accept peace into my life and my daily activities.**

You can assist this mantra to come to fulfillment by visualizing that peace that you desire over and over until it manifests itself. You can make use of this mantra to call peace into any aspect of your life: your mind, your soul, your work etc. When these words are repeated over time, your mind begins to believe them and align towards having them accomplished.

2. **I will strive for the best instead of striving for perfection.**

We have gone through this, and I have explained how toxic perfectionism can be to you and the people around you. Make use of this mantra to overcome a mindset of perfectionism. Before you start an important task, you can repeat it over and over until your mind assimilates it. When you find yourself gradually falling into that mindset of perfectionism, repeat it, and give yourself the required focus.

3. **My mistakes are for my benefits.**

Playing the blame game is always easy, and this mantra is here to help you do the exact opposite of that. Use this mantra when you have made a stupid mistake and feel like you are a failure. Keep it from time to time, even as your mind may try to make you feel bad about the decisions you may have made in the past.

4. **I will focus on my present.**

The mantra is most importantly used when you noticed your mind gradually slipping back to your past or worrying about the future. Remind yourself using this mantra to keep your focus on the present.

5.   **I will meet my deadlines and achieve all my goals.**

Use this mantra at the beginning of each day, first thing after you wake in the morning or while washing your mouth. As you repeat this mantra to yourself, continue to visualize what you accomplished goals will look like. Ruminate over all the exciting benefits open to you as you hit your daily targets.

Conclusion

I want to appreciate you for following me on this journey, for preserving and being here until this moment. In fact, thank you for not procrastinating the reading of this book. I believe you have skipped pages but read through the book with all diligence.

Throughout this book, I have done everything possible to help you understand the concept of procrastination and how it works. We have explored some of the major triggers of procrastination and also the main ways in which you can get over and conquer these triggers. But I can tell you that regardless of the wealth of knowledge hidden in this book, this is not all it takes.

I can tell you that we all face our own different procrastination triggers that are specific to each and every one of us. While reading a book, I am quite certain that you encounter the one that most related to your situation. These are the issues that you need to address as soon as possible. You cannot change everything at once. Try and employ some strategy to your action plan in defeating procrastination.

It is one thing to own the rod, and it is another thing to strike the snake. Most people will go to any length to acquire the rod but will never take action to strike the snake until it bites. I want to tell you that you can break free from the grip of procrastination today, if only you will decide to take action and follow the instructions listed in this book. There will be a point where you will feel like you have failed when it will seem like you should just give up and stop trying, but don't allow that stop you. Promise yourself that you will fight right till the end. Only keep your focus on making some small necessary changes and see your life improve every day.

www.ingramcontent.com/pod-product-compliance
Lightning Source LLC
Chambersburg PA
CBHW031109080526
44587CB00011B/891